EXPRESSIVE SINGING

Dalcroze Eurhythmics
for
Voice

J. Timothy Caldwell

Central Michigan University

PRENTICE HALL, Upper Saddle River, New Jersey 07458

Library of Congress Cataloging-in-Publication Data

CALDWELL, J. TIMOTHY (date)
   Expressive singing : Dalcroze eurhythmics for voice / J. Timothy
Caldwell
      p. cm.
   Includes bibliographical references and index.
   ISBN 0-13-045295-5
   1. Jaques-Dalcroze, Emile, 1865–1950. 2. Musical meter and
rhythm. 3. Musico-callisthenics. 4. Singing—instruction and
study. I. Title.
MT22.C35 1995
783'.04—dc20   94–2030
                                                    CIP
                                                    MN

Acquisitions editor: Bud Therien

Editorial production supervision
    and interior design: F. Hubert

Manufacturing buyer: Bob Anderson

Cover design: Miguel Ortiz

Printed in the United States of America

10 9 8 7 6 5 4 3 2 1

ISBN 0-13-045295-5

Prentice-Hall International (UK) Limited,London
Prentice-Hall of Australia Pty. Limited, Sydney
Prentice-Hall Canada Inc., Toronto
Prentice-Hall Hispanoamericana, S.A., Mexico
Prentice-Hall of India Private Limited, New Delhi
Prentice-Hall of Japan, Inc., Tokyo
Pearson Education Asia Pte. Ltd., Singapore
Editora Prentice-Hall do Brasil, Ltda., Rio de Janeiro

To Barb, with all my love,

and

To Robert Abramson, teacher, friend, mentor:

Thanks for the kick in the pants.

◆ Contents ◆

◆ **PART II** ◆
The Dalcroze Methodology **19**

◆ **Chapter 4** ◆
the Dalcroze equation **21**

◆ **Chapter 5** ◆
the normative measure and its effect **30**

◆ **Chapter 6** ◆
understanding music through kinesthetics **39**

◆ **Chapter 7** ◆
improvisation **45**

◆ **Chapter 8** ◆
rhythmic solfege **56**

◆ Foreword ◆

Hats off, Everyone! Timothy Caldwell gives us a new book with a new vision, new purpose, and new goals. This is not just another book on the art or science of voice production, but it is a practical guide that unites the techniques of voice training to its original and now mostly forgotten purpose: the ability of a singer to project musical feelings and poetic pictures and stories to move a listening audience.

It is interesting that more songs and singers are being taught at more schools in the United States than ever before. Sad to say, this is not leading to either a revival in great performance or even an audience's deeper appreciation of the seventeenth-, eighteenth-, nineteenth-, or twentieth-century song literature. The fact is that fewer people than ever before can sing "Happy Birthday" in tune and in time. Even ordinary speech, just one part of singing, has deteriorated into the expressive realm of the harsh, colorless, and/or emotionless computerlike qualities. One wonders if America is losing its voice and its ear for the folk and art music of the seventeenth, eighteenth, and nineteenth centuries and if anything except the country-western, pop, rock, and disco styles of singing could be authentic means of expression.

Perhaps the solution to the revitalization of the old vocal culture lies in changing the training of singers. At the present time, most of the training is technical and is concerned with building the vocal instrument. This is a worthwhile goal if the student is also gifted with the desire and skill to project musical-poetic expression. However, many students are severely deficient in this talent or skill, and "building a vocal instrument" without building an understanding of expressive technique indicates a certain lack of responsibility on the part of the teacher. This kind of voice education, without a musical education, is something like an architect who draws a plan to put up the foundation and outer walls of a building but does not think out the problems of lighting, heating, and other necessities that will help to make the building warm, livable, friendly, and aesthetically appealing. This same architect leaves it to others to do the basic work. The result of this imbalance in training and limited viewpoint is often a "one sound fits everything" quality so that songs about love, hate, war, sleep, or revenge all sound and feel the same. This training can lead to the "pretty" sound, though the effect is often constipated or pretentious. All of these problems come about from the erroneous belief that vocal technique has nothing to do with musical expression or musical gesture. Though voice production is taught everywhere, musical expression and poetry are not. Musical expression can only be produced by training the student in the nuances, accents, and phrasing of rhythmic movement. Poetic expression can only be produced by training in the appreciation of the colors and rhythmic movements of language.

The coordination of vocal technique and embodied knowledge about musical expression revealed in this book can help teachers and students bridge the gap that all artists and magicians must bridge. I say "artists and magicians" because both must seduce the audience to believe in an illusion of reality and life. Just as the magician creates illusions of a world that does not exist, a singer leads audiences to believe and understand the feelings and ideas that are encoded in the musical score. As long as the techniques of voice production, musicality, and poetry are separated, this cannot be accomplished.

Now that the separation between the concepts of mind, body, and soul is being discarded in the sciences, the time has come to unite and heal the separation between the culture of voice, poetry, and musicality. Timothy Caldwell has undertaken this gigantic task by combining the powers of Emile Jaques-Dalcroze's general exercises in the physical expression of musical rhythm with the specific exercises and examples of the laws of musical expression. By teaching us how to unleash the power of rhythm, which Plato described as the "dance of the soul," Professor Caldwell helps lead the battle for the return of good singing to its rightful place as *expressive singing* responsive to *any style, any language,* using *any text.*

ROBERT M. ABRAMSON
The Juilliard School/The Manhattan School
New York City

◆ Preface ◆

Music is one of the most powerful forces known to humans; it touches us, moves us, opens the doors of our soul's isolation, and for an ineffable moment, allows us to touch the soul of another. The power of music is emotion, a word from the Latin term *exmovere*, which means "to move out of."[1] The expression of emotion in music comes through motion that is felt by the performer and perceived by the listener. Singing is the most personal medium through which music passes, using our bodies to express the mingled feelings of the composer and performer as its power extends to the listener.

I am a performer and voice teacher, and my love of performing is equaled by my love of teaching. I know many other teachers/performers who feel similarly. However, over the years I have grown uneasy that, as teachers, we seem to have become enamored of the creation of wonderful techniques and lost sight of the reason for singing: the expression of thought and feeling. One reason for our focus on technique is that it seems somehow more objective, more obvious, and more accessible to instruction than expression of emotion. Expressing emotion, particularly within a particular musical style (e.g., Baroque, Classical), often seems to be a murky issue, difficult to pin down. Nevertheless, just as a vocal technique can be taught, I believe musical expression can also be taught. Much of the murkiness of expression can be removed if there were guidelines for us to follow. Fortunately, such guidelines exist. They are guidelines governing expression, guidelines that the best performers follow intuitively, and they can be taught.

The question is, What is the best way to teach expression? If, in

---

[1] *Webster's New Collegiate Dictionary* (Springfield, MA: G. & C. Merriam, 1974), p. 372.

fact, the goal of singing is to express emotion,[2] and emotion results from movement, does this mean singers should dance around as they sing in order to convey their feelings? No. Ideally the performer has internalized the "dance" of the music so he or she can stand quietly and sing in such a powerful, "moving" manner that the audience feels compelled to dance and sway. This is real "singer power."[3]

Singers, and teachers of singers, are intuitively attracted to using movement to improve performance, but very few of us are systematically trained in movement or its application. One goal of this book is to introduce you to a century-old methodology that uses movement to teach all elements of music as well as to improve technical performance. The method is called Dalcroze Eurhythmics and bears the name of its creator, Emile Jaques-Dalcroze (1865–1950).

Using concepts from eurhythmics can provide valuable clues into the nature of musical expression. My intention is that the book may serve as a guide in developing expressive techniques whether you are a student, teacher, or performer.

I examine three major issues in the book:

1. The teaching/learning process of studying voice
2. The techniques of expression
3. The methodology of Emile Jaques-Dalcroze and its use in teaching areas 1 and 2

The book has three divisions:

◆ Part I provides a background for what follows in the rest of the book, includes a brief biography of Emile Jaques-Dalcroze, and presents a view of his philosophy and some of the questions he raised that impact on how music could be taught.

◆ Part II explores the three elements of the Dalcrozian methodology, the Dalcroze equation for eurhythmic performance, and explains the types of behavior needed to learn music successfully.

◆ Part III, "Putting the Dalcroze Methodology to Work," describes the teaching/learning process and techniques of expression and presents sample lessons that demonstrate their application. The appendix following Part III serves as a quick reference to exercises and guidelines elaborated on in the text.

---

[2] It may be argued that singing expresses ideas, or tells a story, in addition to expressing a feeling. While I agree, I am compelled to add that the composer uses the content (the information conveyed by the words) to elicit emotion from the listener.

[3] Thanks to Wesley Balk for creating this wonderful term.

Above all, I hope *Expressive Singing: Dalcroze Eurhythmics for Voice* will provide a source of new insights for your teaching and performing and give you new perspectives on our art.

ACKNOWLEDGMENTS

I have been privileged to have many fine teachers, students, and colleagues over the years, and have learned a great deal from them. However, several must be mentioned and thanked here because of the lasting influence they have had on me and my career as a performer and teacher:

◆ First and foremost, I thank Dr. Barbara Dixon, professor of piano and associate dean, College of Arts and Sciences at Central Michigan University, my significant other, friend, and colleague, for her "little suggestions" that changed the direction of my career. She has been, and continues to be, my musical role model.

◆ My fellow voice teachers at Central Michigan University, Mary Stewart Kiesgen, Cora Enman, Jeffrey Foote, and Nina Nash-Robertson, director of choirs, deserve my thanks for their long-suffering support and friendship, even when it appeared I might have gone off the deep end.

◆ The Department of Music at Central Michigan University must be included for allowing me the freedom to move outside the mold of "voice teacher," and into the areas related to teaching and performing. My colleagues, particularly in the areas of music education and piano, have cheerfully aided and abetted me in my Dalcroze studies.

◆ Dr. Julie Meyer deserves special thanks for her careful reading of the manuscript and thoughtful suggestions.

◆ Boris Goldovsky, Director of the Goldovsky Opera, who taught me that the opera score has the stage directions built into the music. He also insisted that opera should be believable: a radical concept.

◆ H. Wesley Balk, former Artistic Director of the Minnesota Opera, whose genius is putting together all the performance elements and providing ways to train the singer/actor.

◆ Dr. Guy Duckworth, emeritus professor of piano pedagogy, College of Music, University of Colorado, Boulder. His cogent insight into the teaching/learning process as well as his profound understanding of music continue to influence my teaching and performing.

The teachers with whom I studied voice through the years have greatly influenced this book:

◆ John McCollum, professor of voice, University of Michigan, shepherded me through my undergraduate and master's degrees and instilled in me the love of singing recitals and bringing them to dramatic life.

◆ The late Gene Greenwell, professor of voice, Michigan State University, provided me with conscious technical choices and helped me learn to listen to my students with my "technical ears" on.

◆ Dr. Barbara Doscher, professor of voice, College of Music, University of Boulder, Colorado, refined and enhanced my technique during our short year together.

◆ Walter Blazer, emeritus professor of voice, the Manhattan School of Music, and Maria Blazer, with whom I had very few lessons, but their encouragement of my performing and their dedication to teaching continue to be felt and appreciated.

◆ Finally, Robert Abramson, professor of rhythmics, The Juilliard School, who has been called the premier Dalcroze teacher of the latter part of the twentieth century. It is a title he rightfully holds. He has also been called the "transformer" because that is what he does. He has changed the way I look at and listen to music, as well as the way I teach and perform, and I am just one of hundreds of musicians he has transformed through the years. He is a man of great love and passion, and I am proud to count him as a friend.

J. TIMOTHY CALDWELL

◆ PART I ◆

Background

The experience of art is personal; the experience of teaching is just as personal. Chapter 1 begins with an abbreviated summary of the "journey" I have made over my twenty years of teaching. It is included not because it is unique (although for me it was), but rather because it is so typical. Many of the questions that arose out of my experiences are typical as well because I have heard my colleagues ask them over the years.

Chapter 2 continues with an examination of several ideas which are commonly held among voice teachers and performers. The section concludes with Chapter 3, a historical overview of the life and thought of Emile Jaques-Dalcroze, the developer of the method known in the United States as *Eurhythmics*.

◆ Chapter 1 ◆

one
voice teacher's
education

In my travels as a singer and clinician, I have found many other teacher/performers who share my background: we received performance degrees and found employment in educational institutions because of our performance abilities, not our teaching skills. In our new positions, we took on the role of voice teacher in a state of mind that might be described as "controlled terror" because we realized we had not been taught to teach. We had taken the pedagogy classes but usually, even in the most prestigious schools, the classes taught under the rubric of vocal pedagogy dealt with anatomy and acoustics, but little was said about the subject of learning theories, teaching and learning styles, or technique as a means to expressive performing.

The pedagogy teachers apparently assumed we all knew how to teach music, since we were all musicians. Acoustics and anatomy are relatively concrete and the information is easier to communicate than issues such as what constitutes musical styles or expressive performance. Hence most of us began teaching as we were taught (or how we thought we were taught) and continued the teaching traditions that were passed to us.

Once we were on our own with our own students, or preparing our own performances, we discovered our education was just beginning. We attended master classes to learn new "teaching tips." There we listened as Madame Z told us how she preferred the last four measures of Lucia's Mad Scene be sung, and insisted they should always be performed that way, since that was what her coach taught her. Or how Professor Y discovered through oscilloscope experiments that by dropping the jaw, touching the right cheek with the tongue, and forming the vowel i^1,

---

[1] I will use the International Phonetic Alphabet for all examples of pronunciation.

tenors can sing an *a* at mezzo forte on high B-flat. We learned from work-shops in "creative teaching" that by standing on her head while waving her arms and feet, a young mezzo-soprano could free her voice to sing thirty-six measures of "Voi che sapete" in one breath without fainting.

We would rush back to our studios armed with these fresh "tips," eager to try them on our students without understanding the principles that had been used in the master classes. Predictably, the new tips en-abled our students to make only short-lived technical changes or, more often, failed outright. Looking back on my experiences and the accounts of others, I have realized the failure was due not so much to the fault of the new teaching technique (although Professor Y's approach is ques-tionable), but to a lack of understanding about the technique's effect on the music. I began to understand that we teachers supposedly attended master classes to improve our teaching, but most of us were really only interested in new gimmicks to add to our teaching, and were not moti-vated to examine what and how we taught.

We read books on vocal pedagogy, but found that most of them dealt with diction, vowel usage, muscular use, acoustics, and related is-sues while mentioning in passing "expressive singing." Seldom, if ever, did any of the books examine that mysterious, murky realm.

If your experience was similar to mine, then obviously something was missing. As I attended concerts, I began to pay attention to my reac-tions and the behavior of other members of the audience. Even at recitals presented by well-known singers, I often found myself counting the lights in the ceiling after several pieces. My mind would drift off. When I looked around the audience, I saw inert bodies and glazed eyes—not ex-actly signs of deep emotional involvement.

Why such unresponsiveness during the performances? The singers' techniques were usually superb, their voices often had a seamless quality from the lowest to the highest notes, they could sing very high (or very low), and very loud and very fast; some sang softly occasionally. From time to time, I could even understand some of the words.

On even rarer occasions, I heard a singer who had all the qualities just mentioned and something extra that made me pay constant atten-tion, something which touched me and changed me. In groping to de-scribe this extra quality, I realized I kept referring not only to the beauty of the singer's voice but the way the voice expressed his or her feelings about the music. Technique was present, but it served to illuminate the expressive elements of the music instead of calling attention to itself.

I experienced similar reactions as I listened to recordings of my own performances. I seemed connected to some pieces and not to others; sometimes the singing moved me, and at other times I seemed to struggle with a piece, not necessarily because of technical problems, but as if I were engaged not in a dance, but rather a vocal/musical wrestling match.

What was happening during those moments when the audience and I were moved by the performance? What was missing when we were not moved? Part of the answer occurred to me one day as I watched an Olympic gymnastics event. I realized that I was excited and impressed by the coordination, spirit, concentration, discipline, and beauty of form I witnessed, but I did not mistake it for art. Why? For example, ballet and other forms of dance possess all the qualities of gymnastics, but we place them in the category of art because their goal (at least theoretically) is expression of the affect (emotion) of the music they depict. The greatest performers in any musical medium are remembered not only for their phenomenal technique, but for what they expressed with that technique. How they shaped their sounds gave the impression of movement through space, of music that moved. Their ability to move sounds through space is to be found in their expressive techniques.

The function of Western music is to distract us, overwhelm us, calm us, arouse us, give us a sense of grandeur, awe, fear, hate, beauty, ugliness, hope, joy, despair; you name the emotion, and a piece has probably been composed which expresses that emotion. Yet if technique remains the primary focus of teaching, with only a nod at the expressive elements of the music, then the outcome is inexpressive singing: the medium (technique) becomes the message, and art becomes mere gymnastics.

What if musical expressiveness were taught along with technique? What if expressiveness was, in fact, the key to developing technique? I wish the idea of developing technique through musical understanding had originated with me, but alas, Jaques-Dalcroze and other teachers proposed such teaching in the nineteenth century. This is not an issue of teaching expressiveness instead of technique (expressiveness versus technique), but rather which one receives the primary focus in most lessons.

Much of today's vocal training is similar to horse-drawn wagons in that we teachers and performers have the cart before the horse: the cart is the vocal mechanism, diction, and so on; the horse represents the sensibilities and emotional expressiveness of the composer and performer that inform and lead the technique. We need both the cart and the horse to get anywhere, but having the cart *behind* the horse makes for an easier journey.

THE ECLECTIC VOICE TEACHER

Psychologists, like voice teachers, are people who often describe themselves as professionally eclectic. However, the best psychologists usually can point to one school of therapy they are trained in, which they use as a reference system. This school provides the therapist with a structured way of seeing and hearing the information the client provides, and suggests a structured process for helping the client.

We voice teachers, however, seldom leave the eclectic category because we do not have a structured process for teaching our students to perform expressively. We do have schools of thought about issues like these:

The "white" sound, the "black" sound, the "German" sound, "French" sound, "Italian" sound, the "pop" sound.

Diction: "to roll or not to roll" the R's in German. Should we use consonants or not? Do vowels really migrate or should we leave that to ducks and geese?

And, the granddaddy of them all, vocal technique. Technical schools of thought argue questions like: What does "support" mean? Can you really "place" the voice? Do registers exist, and if so, how many?

There are even voice teachers who maintain they don't teach singing but, rather, "build voices," leaving the musical side to coaches.

Why aren't teachers taught how to teach expression? There are several reasons. The first is that traditional teaching accepts the myth that expressive singers are born, not made, while almost anyone can be taught to use their larynges better.

I agree that each generation produces a few singers who seem born with innate understanding in one area of performance, for example, opera. However, listening to any one singer in various roles in operas from different periods and languages usually leaves the impression that all the music sounds alike and merely serves as a vehicle for a glorious voice because of the unchanging sound of the singing. Listening to that same glorious voice in another genre, for example, lied or oratorio, often proves disappointing because having a glorious voice does not guarantee an expressive performance in other styles.

Another justification for not·teaching expressive singing is put forth by teachers who describe themselves as "voice builders." They contend that singing with "feeling" gets in the way of solid technique. However, even these teachers have the students sing literature during lessons, perhaps giving the students the unfortunate impression that singing is about producing correct vowels on given pitches at the right time.

I liken this philosophy (first technique, expression later) to what my father was told as a child: "Don't go in the water until you know how to swim." Naturally, he never learned to swim. Rather than omitting the expressive elements until technique is solid and the musical score is learned, it is preferable to deal with all three challenges at the same time. After all, this is what the performer has to do in actual performance. It is sometimes necessary to focus on technique, but if we dwell on technique too long, we might drown if we jump into the sea of affect.

WHY THE DALCROZE METHOD?

If you are a teacher, imagine creating situations where students show you what they hear. If you are a student, imagine having your body demonstrate, for example, that it does not understand the phrasing of a composition, so, through movement, you learn the structure of the piece *without constantly singing*. Using the concepts of Dalcroze Eurhythmics offers possibilities for creating awareness of what our bodies "hear" and understand, as well as providing means for melding vocal technique with deliberate techniques of expression.

The Dalcroze method is the oldest, and least understood, of the modern systems of music education. It is also the only one that is directly applied to improving performance. No one system is a panacea for all our musical and technical problems, but the Dalcroze method is, I believe, as near as we have come. It is a system that incorporates (literally, since *incorporate* means to "put into a body") all the elements of music, kinesthetics, the teaching/learning process, affect, and improvisation. The uses for these ideas are limited only by our imagination and musicianship.

◆ Chapter 2 ◆

vocal

mythology

Before looking at the method of Eurhythmics and its applications, these three vocal myths need to be examined:

1. Musically expressive singers are born, not made.
2. Developing vocal technique and learning music have to be separate functions.
3. Music making is about accurate pitches, rhythms, clear diction, and good technique.

I use the term *myths* as Joseph Campbell and other mythologists define the term, that is, ideas that might or might not be based on fact or actual historical events, but are held in common by members of a society and are used to define their world and give meaning to their lives (Campbell, pp. 4–5). Voice teachers, like any other subculture, have certain ideas that have been passed from one generation to the next, ideas we accept as true because "everyone" believes them.

Like many other myths, each myth listed here is a mixture of one part fact and two parts unexamined premises.

◆ Myth 1
Musically expressive singers are born, not made.

This belief might be summarized as "you either got it or you ain't." As I listen to singers, I am constantly amazed by the miracle of being able to produce sounds that other people are interested in hearing. Compared to the entire population of the world, only a very small, very elite group, in any society, can rightfully be called "singers." However, even in that small group, most possess average voices and musical abilities. As teachers who are not clairvoyant, we cannot accurately predict which of those average singers who walk through our studio doors will evolve into outstanding performers once their technical and musical problems have been resolved. Unfortunately, as voice teachers, most of us are better equipped to deal with technique; we prefer to rely on vocal coaches (if such a rare creature dwells nearby) to deal with musical expression. If we were discussing dancing, this would be tantamount to being a dance instructor who only dealt with left legs. Just as dance study is more productive if dancers are allowed to use *both* legs, so singers need to use both "legs" of singing: vocal technique and musical expression.

It is difficult to teach or perform expressively if "expression" is not well understood. While no one person can claim to know everything about what constitutes expressive performance, we can begin to study what qualities expressive performances, and expressive performers, have in common. These expressive elements (techniques) can then be analyzed, codified, and taught. Providing ways for the teacher and performer to identify, analyze, and correct musical problems is part of the rationale for writing this book.

◆ **Myth 2**
Developing vocal technique and learning music have to be separate functions.

This myth sounds true only because it has become common practice. There are teachers who believe teaching music is about teaching technique, and the blossoming music industry called "voice science" has come into being over the last fifteen years based on this myth. Advocates of this thinking, calling themselves *vocal scientists* and *voice builders*, are conducting fascinating research in the acoustical and muscular aspects of voice production. Voice teachers need to know about such things, but music is more than mere technique.

I performed a recital several years ago for an audience that included a well-known vocal scientist, Dr. X. After the program, Dr. X passed through the receiving line and commented, "Your *i*'s and *u*'s were quite good, however keep working on the [^] in your upper voice." An acquaintance of mine, standing in line behind Dr. X, immediately remarked to me, "Did Dr. X hear any of the music?" No, Dr. X heard only a succession of vowel sounds.

The premise that teaching voice is primarily about teaching technique does not take into account the possibility that the music and musical expression inform the technique. Singers who develop only one technical approach tend to perform all styles in the same manner. Recently, internationally acclaimed operatic singers have begun recording songs from popular musicals. Their voices are wonderful, but they insist on using the same technical approach that made them famous on the operatic stage. However, the popular music they are recording requires a different vocal and musical approach. The resulting recordings sound uncomfortable. They are the aural equivalent of the overweight middle-aged man struggling to fit into the clothes he wore as a teenager; he might be able to squeeze into them, but no one wants to be around when he tries to sit down.

I write this not so much to criticize the dubious choices made by these singers, but to point out the results of singing all styles with one technical approach. A thorough background in technique should enable the singer to give authentic performances in several styles. Singers need strong techniques, so there will always be the need for technical studies. However, consider what could happen if voice lessons became studies in technique *and* musical expression.

I define vocal technique as *the preparation of the vocal instrument, and the mind that controls it, for expressing musical thought*. While there are appropriate times to separate technical and musical requirements, to continuously keep them separate can lead to treating literature as if it were a kind of extended vocalise. If music is meant to tell stories and ideas, and express related feelings, then singing, which is perhaps the original way of making music, is the most direct and powerful of the performance mediums because the sound comes directly from a human body. I believe the goal of technique is to prepare the mind and body to serve the music. Excellent teaching results in secure vocal technique linked with an understanding of methods of musical expression; excellent performance is the public presentation of the melding of vocal and expressive techniques.

◆ **Myth 3**
Music making is about accurate pitches, rhythms, clear diction, and good technique.

Of course pitch, rhythm, diction, and technique are all necessary elements in performance. However, they do not constitute the final expressive performance if they are not held together by an emotive "glue." There is a theory in gestalt research stating that the whole is greater than the sum of the parts. An expressive performer uses the elements of pitch, rhythm, diction, and technique to create the rhythmic "dance" that generates the emotional milieu for the music, whereas the inexpressive performer makes one or more of the elements the goal of the performance. How often have you heard a performer struggle for "correctness" while you and others in the audience were bored to tears?

Expressive singing is more than a collection of vowel sounds, technical accomplishments, accurate score reading, or even clear diction. The historical raison d'être of singing has been, and continues to be, a means of expressing musical thought and feeling. But what constitutes expression, and how do you learn to sing expressively? What are these guidelines and techniques that can lead to expressive singing? Emile Jaques-Dalcroze provided many of the answers to these questions at the beginning of the twentieth century.

◆ Chapter 3 ◆

Emile Jaques-Dalcroze

BIOGRAPHY

Emile Jaques was born in Vienna in 1865 of Swiss parents living in Austria. Emile showed unusual abilities as a pianist at an early age and was taught by his mother, a music teacher who had studied the philosophy and techniques of Johann Heinrich Pestalozzi (1746–1827), a Swiss educational innovator. Under her guidance, Emile and his sister Hélène sang duets and played four-hand piano compositions from a very early age. He wrote his first march for the piano at age seven, and the first of more than 600 songs he would write during his lifetime.

His parents returned to Geneva when he was seven, and he was enrolled in the Conservatory of Music and the College of Geneva. After graduating, he moved to Paris to study composition with Léo Delibes and Gabriel Fauré, and to study acting with members of the Comédie Française. In 1885 Emile returned to Geneva where he studied with Mathis Lussy, a Swiss theorist. Lussy's theories for teaching rhythm and musical expression were to profoundly influence Dalcroze's later work in those areas.

Emile was achieving some success as a composer, and it was during this time that one of his publishers suggested he change his name to something less common so his compositions would be more easily remembered. So he created the name "Dalcroze" (an acquaintance of Emile's had the name "Valcroze" and allowed Emile to use his name with this little variation) and became Emile Jaques-Dalcroze (his books may be found in libraries under Jaques-Dalcroze).

He spent 1886 in Algiers as an assistant conductor at the Algiers opera and discovered Arabic music with its irregular and intricate rhythms. He later wrote that it was during his short conducting career that he discovered gesture and music must be integrated. He returned to Vienna in 1887 and enrolled in the Vienna Conservatory to study composition with Anton Bruckner. After graduation, he returned to Geneva with a broad background as a pianist, actor, conductor, singer, composer, and poet, and was appointed professor of harmony and solfege at the Conservatory of Music in Geneva in 1893, when he was twenty-eight.

Jaques-Dalcroze quickly discovered his students at the conservatory could not hear the harmonies they were writing in theory classes, were unable to write a simple melody or chord sequence, and that they had serious problems in their performance because of a poorly developed rhythmic sense. So he discarded the ear training texts and introduced a new subject: improvisation. He realized the students did not feel at home with much of their music, so he encouraged them to express themselves vocally or on the piano at the spur of the moment and experience music as a language of the emotions. He pondered the close connection between acoustics, nerve centers, and muscular movement, and decided that musicality, if purely aural, was not complete unless muscles could coordinate with the music. He began to study ways in which music, movement, cognition, and physical skills were related and realized the missing link, the force that bound thought, imagination, and physical skills, was kinesthetics.[1]

The conservatory authorities were not interested in his newfangled theories, so in 1893 he rented a studio and, with the help of student volunteers, began experimenting with studying music through movement. The principles he developed with his students were so original that they were given special names: in Europe, *Le Rythme*; in Asia, *Dalcroze-Rhythmics*; and *Eurhythmics* in England and North America.

He began his experiments simply, much the way Eurhythmics teachers begin today, by having the students step to the music he improvised. These exercises eventually included all the elements of music: note values, measures, rhythmic patterns, phrases, polyrhythms, group work, and conducting. Improvisation was a part of every lesson. Learning and creating were in constant interplay: students would invent rhythms, perform them physically, melodically, harmonically, and develop them in many ways, then write and read them. There were basic physical exercises with specific studies in muscular sensitivity controlled by sound, and studies in breathing and relaxation were developed to prepare the body for fluid, harmonious movement.

By 1905 he and his students were ready to present the complete methodology of Eurhythmics: rhythmic solfege, improvisation, and rhythmics. Jaques-Dalcroze understood that people tend to learn and remember more when they enjoy the process of learning. Therefore he

[1]*Thesia* is a Greek term for "awareness of." Therefore kinesthesia (kines-thesia) literally means "awareness of motion."

taught musical concepts by using activities he described as "games" or "exercises." Present-day Dalcroze teachers continue to use the term *games*.

As he and his troupe traveled throughout Europe, his ideas were received warmly by many performers and teachers although others, in more rigid academic settings, opposed them, because Eurhythmics was an entirely new approach to learning music. Jaques-Dalcroze did have very important admirers in two brothers named Dhorn. The Dhorns were German industrialists and advocates of social reform. Because of their interest in Jaques-Dalcroze's work, they built an institute for him at Hellerau near Dresden, Germany, in 1910. Eventually several hundred students from fourteen nations lived and studied there.

Jaques-Dalcroze's early work reached its climax at Hellerau in 1913 with performances of Gluck's opera *Orfeo*. All the participants—singers, orchestra, set designer, and choreographer—had been trained in Jaques-Dalcroze's new methodology, so movement, music, light, and space were in complete harmony.

More than five thousand people from around the world attended the festival. Major names in theater, dance, and literature attended, such as Stanislawski, Nijinski, Diaghilev, G. B. Shaw, and Upton Sinclair. Almost overnight, Hellerau became a world center for education through the arts. Eurhythmics was introduced into theaters, dance schools, and educational institutions around the world, and Dalcroze training schools opened in many countries.

This era ended abruptly in 1914 with the onset of the First World War. Hellerau closed and Jaques-Dalcroze returned to Geneva where he opened a new school in 1915. The two world wars isolated Switzerland and severely limited Jaques-Dalcroze's influence outside that country. However, he continued his work and on his seventieth birthday he received a book containing 10,500 signatures of former students representing forty-six nationalities. He lived to see his methodology used in public schools, conservatories of music, colleges, schools of opera and theater, and in therapeutic work with the blind, deaf, and mentally and physically handicapped children and adults.

Emile Jaques-Dalcroze died in 1950. The institute in Geneva that bears his name continues to train Dalcroze teachers from around the world.

INFLUENCES

Jaques-Dalcroze and his methodology can hardly be discussed without at least a nod in the direction of the teachers who influenced him: Johann Heinrich Pestalozzi, Edouard Claparède, and Mathis Lussy.

Pestalozzi, as mentioned earlier, was a Swiss educator whose theories would eventually influence Lowell Mason (1792–1872), who is credited with establishing music education in public schools in the United States, and John Dewey (1859–1952), who some call the father of public education in the United States. Pestalozzi was the first influential educator to reject the school practices of rote memorization and recitation, calling instead for teachers to create conditions in which the students learn through observation, experimentation, and reasoning. His credo was "Read nothing: Discover everything: Prove all things." He insisted on teaching the "whole child: mentally, physically, and morally," "training the head, hand, and heart" (Choksy, p. 5).

Mathis Lussy (1828–1910), with whom Jaques-Dalcroze worked as a student in Geneva, had the novel opinion that good composers obey certain expressive "rules" and write them into their compositions. He maintained that composers assume the performer understands these rules; but unfortunately, this is not so. In the 1800s, Lussy protested against dull performances that did little more than serve as showcases for brilliant technique. He believed students could be taught those rules the composers followed, so he codified them, taught them to his students, and insisted they follow them when performing. By following Lussy's rules, the performer could analyze a musical composition for expressive elements while simultaneously learning the words, form, and melodic lines. Thus expressiveness was built into the technique. Jaques-Dalcroze's musical rules are his variations on the numerous rules that Lussy formulated.

Edouard Claparède (1873–1940), who incidentally was the founder of Institut Jean-Jacques Rousseau for the study of child development and a teacher of Jean Piaget, worked closely with Jaques-Dalcroze to develop a systematic approach to the entire teaching process Jaques-Dalcroze used. Jaques-Dalcroze drew from these three sources, Pestalozzi, Lussy, Claparède, and added his own experiences to evolve the principles on which to base his system.

FIRST PRINCIPLES

As mentioned earlier, Jaques-Dalcroze was already an established performer when he was appointed professor of harmony and solfege at the Conservatory of Music in Geneva. In the nineteenth century, the subjects of harmony and solfege included theory, harmony, ear training, sight-singing, and dictation.

He soon realized that there were serious problems with the accepted modes of teaching music. Music theory and notation were taught as abstractions, divorced from the sounds, feelings, and motions they represented. Most music studies were fragmented and specialized; a student attended classes in specialized areas (music theory, music history, music literature, sight-singing/ear training, lessons in a performance medium, etc.) without ever understanding how the music of a particular period was affected by the society, which in turn influenced the aesthetic and theoretical ideals of the composers. Jaques-Dalcroze wondered why so many textbooks on harmony, transposition, and counterpoint were written in an abstract, technical style and were not concerned with developing the skill to hear the effects they described. In the music classes, he saw few teachers who displayed the characteristics of real musicians. He was particularly concerned that in music lessons, students were permitted or required to perform without understanding, read without comprehension, and write what they could not hear or feel (Choksy, pp. 29–30). Remember, this was in the nineteenth century; we are ending the twentieth and the same problems are with us.

In his ruminations, he kept searching for what philosophers call "first principles," those concepts that form the foundation on which philosophical and conceptual frameworks may be built. He asked these questions (Choksy, p. 31):

1. *What is the source of music; where does it begin?* The beginning of music happens when human emotions are translated into musical motion.

2. *Where do we sense emotions?* We experience emotions physically.

3. *How do we sense emotions?* Through sensations of various muscular contractions and releases in our bodies.

4. *How does the body express these internal emotions to the outer world?* By externalizing affect through movements, postures, gestures, and sounds. Some of these are automatic (such as sweaty palms, butterflies in the stomach), some are spontaneous, and others are the results of thought and will.

5. *How are these internal emotions translated into music?* Through motions such as taking a breath, vibrating the vocal folds or having our fingers push pistons or keys on a keyboard.

6. *What, then, is the first instrument that must be trained in music?* The human body! It is not enough to train the fingers, or voice, or ear, or mind; the entire body must be trained, since it has all the essentials for the development of sensibility, sensitivity, and analysis of sound and feeling. Jaques-Dalcroze postulated that any musical idea could be performed by the body (sound becoming gesture), and any movement of the body could be transformed into a musical idea (gesture into sound). He concluded there must be an immediate reaction between the mind that conceives and the body that reacts (Chosky, p. 31).

Consider the questions this raises for us as voice teachers and performers:

◆ What would be the effect of training the entire body (instead of just the vocal folds) to respond to musical thought?

◆ What if we developed our artistic sensibilities as we developed our techniques?

◆ What would happen if we became more interested in the effect of sound instead of the production of sound?

◆ What if we could learn to hear and feel our music internally *before* making it audible?

◆ What if we could hear not only our solo lines, but the harmonies and rhythms that surround and support the lines?

The principles Dalcroze formulated have the potential to fundamentally change the teaching of voice. The key to the Dalcroze approach is movement (kinesthetics). Though we acknowledge we do not sing from just the neck up, few of us have been taught to use movement to learn the "dance" of the music. Instead, we simply stand in place (I am speaking about rehearsals and lessons, not operatic performances) trying to make our vocal muscles work in a kind of physical limbo, as if those microscopic vocal muscles were not connected to the rest of our bodies. What if we could learn to interpret scores as directions for movement, thereby creating moving sounds?

From these and other questions, Jaques-Dalcroze developed a new method of music instruction.

◆ PART II ◆

The

Dalcroze

Methodology

In 1906, Jaques-Dalcroze had his first volumes of work published by Sandoz, Jobin in Paris, and Neuchâtel in Leipzig, under the title *Méthode Jaques-Dalcroze. Pour le développement de l'instinct rhythmique, du sens aduitif et du sentiment tonal, en 5 parties* (Spector, p. 115). Although the word *method* appeared in the title (much to his chagrin), Jaques-Dalcroze insisted his work was not to be seen as a rigid method, but rather as a guide for teachers and students to use as they wish. He advocated that each teacher and student develop original exercises and ideas, and use his examples simply to prime the pump of imagination.

Eurhythmics may be defined as follows: "Eurhythmics . . . is . . . based on the premise that rhythm is the primary element of music, and that the source for all musical rhythm may be found in the natural rhythms of the body" (Choksy, p. 27). All music begins with a gesture on the part of the performer. The gesture originates from the music the performer hears internally and from the degree of control the performer has over the gesture. A eurhythmics teacher endeavors to train the mind that perceives the music, the ear that hears it, and the body that performs it. Eurhythmics uses three approaches:

- ◆ Solfege (to study scales, harmony, and theory)
- ◆ Improvisation (to activate and meld the internal ear and the body)
- ◆ Rhythmics (to explore the external and internal effects of rhythmic gesture in teaching the other two elements)

Since I have not intended this book as a textbook on the Dalcroze system per se, but rather of practical use to you, I give a general overview of the system instead of describing it in great detail. The emphasis is on its application in singing. You will find some exercises and guidelines for expression (occasionally referred to as musical rules), but please bear in mind that they are descriptive rather than prescriptive, and presented as guides for your thinking.

◆ Chapter 4 ◆

the

Dalcroze

equation

What is rhythm? After years of experiments, Jaques-Dalcroze came to define rhythm as "the varieties of flow through space" (Martin, p. 21). Accordingly, he devised an equation that describes the major components of rhythm:

$$\frac{\text{Space} + \text{Time} + \text{Energy} + \text{Weight} + \text{Balance} + \text{Plasticity}}{\text{Gravity}} = \text{Eurhythmia}$$

Of the three elements of music (pitch, rhythm, dynamics), rhythm and dynamics are dependent on motion. The Dalcroze equation describes the elements which, taken together, give the motions involved in rhythmic performance their "quality." *Eurhythmia* (good *[eu]* rhythm *[flow]*) in music occurs when the components of the equation are balanced. The way a composer balances these elements, along with harmonic and melodic progressions, results in what we refer to as the composer's *style*. Every generation of composers used each of these elements in a way that reflected the prevailing sentiments, architecture (the organized use of space), art, and even fashions of the era in which they lived. The heavy attire of the early baroque (some dresses of the period weighed 70 pounds or more), as well as the high heels worn by the men, created a different use of the space, weight, and time inherent in the music. However, the composers of a given period each experience the balance of space, time, energy, plasticity, weight, and balance slightly differently, even though they may follow the musical conventions of their period. This knowledge allows us, when listening to a composition we do not know, to identify not only the era in which a piece was written, but also the probable composer.

The Dalcroze equation raises an interesting question: What flows through space? The answer is matter, which has density and mass. Science tells us that matter is energy made visible because all matter is made of atomic and subatomic particles of energy. Look around you. All the objects you see, the eyes with which you see, the hands with which you touch, are all made of uncountable particles of energy.

SPACE, ENERGY, AND PLASTICITY

> Hold your hands in front of you about two feet apart, palms facing each other. Clap them together at different speeds, being sure to return to the original starting points.

Notice the different levels of energy you used and the changes in time as your hands came together very quickly, then very slowly, then at a speed between the two extremes. Now vary the space between your hands as you change tempos. This is a quick study of the effects of varying time and energy as they move through space.

When matter (energy) is propelled through space, we call this *motion*. There are packets of motion in music called *beats*. Beats release their energy in many ways, for example, quickly, with a sudden surge, or slowly, similar to the ways you clapped your hands. The way a beat releases its motion/energy is called its *quality*.

> Once again, clap your hands together several times at one speed. Now, at the same tempo, slide your hands together several times; bring the backs of your hands together several times; slide your palms together several times; bring the tips of your index fingers together several times. Now do one of each: clap, index fingers, backs-of-hands, slide palms together.

What you have just experienced, in a crude manner, is the effect of varying the quality of beats. Notice how you varied the level of **energy** to change the quality. You used your muscles in different ways to produce the different gestures, so two of the gestures, the touching of the fingers and backs of hands, were probably quieter, while the clap and slide were probably louder. The term *energy* is synonymous with dynamics, but also includes the physical sensation of the change of weight.

Perform the exercise again, but reverse the dynamics. What did you discover about the way you used your muscles?

Take any one of the qualities you just used (clap, index fingers, backs-of-hands, slide palms together) and repeat it sixteen times. Boring, isn't it?

Now use all four of the qualities in various combinations, for sixteen beats. More interesting? This is because you changed the quality of the beats by varying the *plasticity*. It isn't art, but it isn't boring and mechanical. Unfortunately, the first way you performed the exercise (using only one level of energy and plasticity) is the way we often hear entire pieces performed!

The quality of the beat (the way it gives off its energy) affects the voyage of the energy as it moves to the next beat. The voyage between beats moves through space with energy and plasticity. This brings us back to the "varieties of flow" mentioned in the definition of rhythm. Many composers have grumbled over the centuries that not only are the pitches important in their music, but another, intangible quality is vital as well: the movement *between* the pitches.

TIME

The beats are perceived as having duration (length). Plasticity (how the beat is approached, sustained, and released) is an integral part and function of the quality **time**.

Repeat the second exercise under Space, Energy, and Plasticity (clap, index fingers, and so on). Change the order (e.g., slide palms together, index fingers, clap, back of hands). Change the dynamics.

Did you discover that you tended to vary the tempo (time) as you changed the order (plasticity) and/or the dynamics (energy)?

Perform the same exercise *forte*. Perform the exercise *pianissimo*.

Turn on your metronome and perform the exercise above.

What did you discover about the tempo (time)? Most people have difficulty keeping the same tempo while varying the dynamics because they have linked *time* and *energy* so closely that if one changes, the other changes. The tendency is to slow down if the music grows soft, and accelerate if the music becomes louder. This is an indication that the element of energy is overcoming the element of time; the balance between the two has been lost. If you had trouble with the exercise, practice with your metronome until you can vary the dynamics while keeping the tempo steady.

WEIGHT

Mass has weight in a field of gravity. We may also perceive sounds as having a quality of *weight*.

Say the word *thud* strongly, in the lower part of your speaking range. Now say *feather* in a breathy voice, in a higher part of your speaking range. Repeat the words in this manner several times. Pay attention to your responses.

Reverse the words, saying *feather* strongly, in the lower part of your speaking range, and *thud* in a breathy voice, in a higher part of your speaking range.

Saying the words in this manner usually sounds and feels quite strange because the native English speaker intuitively associates the quality of lightness with "feather" and heaviness with "thud." This is what is meant by the statement that sounds may be perceived as having weight. A collection of pitches, such as a chord, is perceived as heavier than a single-voice line. Pitch duration also influences the illusion of weight.

BALANCE

Balance, that is, keeping a mass under control in a field of gravity, is another vital element of rhythm.

Perform this exercise cautiously. Clear a space around you so you can take several steps in any direction. Close your eyes and take three steps forward, turn quickly, and take three steps back to your starting point.

Pay attention to any problems you had keeping your balance, particularly as you turned. In a musical sense, balance enables the performer to change direction, start, stop, speed up, slow down, and juggle the musical elements necessary to produce a successful performance.

Many Dalcroze games are based on the Dalcroze equation. The elements of rhythm are inseparable, but the games allow us to highlight each one in order to increase our understanding of how it functions in a particular piece.

Try this experiment:

> **Slowly clap your hands several times in your normal manner.**

Notice the place where your hands come together is probably the same location in space.

> **Clasp your hands in front of you and draw an imaginary line, moving from left to right. Place four equidistant points on the line with the first point being on your far left. The line might resemble the picture below:**

◆ Illustration 4-1 ◆

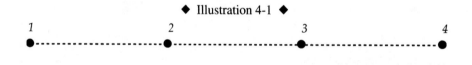

> **Clap four times again, moving from the first point to the last, arching your hands from 4 back to 1 as you repeat the pattern several times.**

◆ Illustration 4-2 ◆

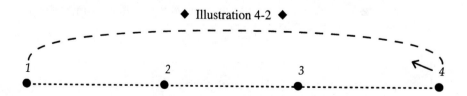

What does it feel like to move through space?

> Go back to your normal clapping again. Now back to the new pattern. Alternate these patterns several times.

What do you experience as the difference between these two ways of clapping? Whatever your answer(s), as you varied your movement, you changed your kinesthetics.

Maybe you experienced the difference between the movements, with your normal way of clapping feeling mechanical, while the new way had more of a liquid, flowing quality. The mechanical quality is described as *er*rhythmic and the flowing quality as *eu*rhythmic.

> Now, keeping your tempo the same as in the first two experiments, move your hands between your imaginary points in different ways.

◆ Illustration 4-3 ◆

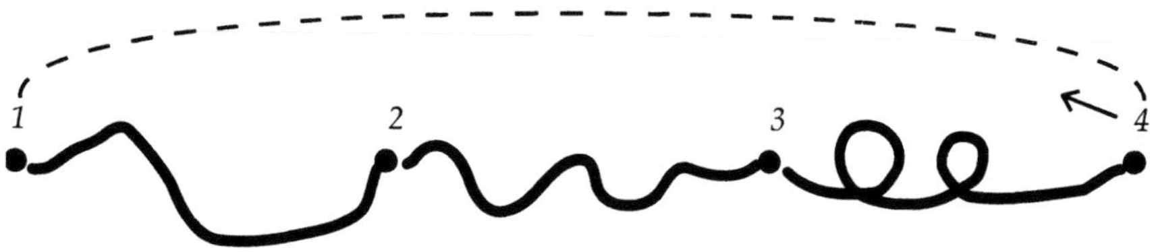

> Find other ways to move between the four points, being sure to keep the same tempo.

What you are discovering is the *feeling* of rhythm, that is, "the varieties of flow through space."

Time is an aspect of the speed in which an object moves through space between two points. An object moving a short distance requires less energy to reach its goal, just as an object moving a longer distance requires greater energy to reach its goal.

> Repeat Illustration 4-2. Without changing the space, be attentive to how long it takes your hand to move from one point to another. Now perform the exercise twice as fast. Double your speed again.

Do you find you tend to tighten the muscles in your hand, or arm, or shoulder (maybe all three) as you move faster? This is performance tension. Repeat the exercise but without the tension.

> **Perform the exercise rapidly again, but this time reduce the space by half.**

What you experience?

> **Return to the original amount of space for the exercise. Continue to work at your fastest speed, but reduce the amount of mass that has to move. If you originally moved your entire arm, now allow most of your arm to be quiet as you move only your forearm, wrist, and fingers between the points in space.**

This exercise points out the importance of using less mass when moving faster, and the effect of space on time, energy, weight, and balance.

Performers who are effective in balancing the elements of the equation will not hurt themselves performing. An entire field of arts medicine, rather like sports medicine, has emerged within the last few years because more and more performers are unable to balance the elements in the Dalcroze equation. They also spend too much of their time practicing, singing when they should be listening and thinking, thus becoming future patients for arts doctors.

The Dalcroze equation is a tool that not only helps us perform and teach music better, but can actually help the physical act of performing. How often have you heard a singer who was tying his larynx in knots trying to sing a melismatic passage due to singing too loudly (with too much energy), or too heavily (with too much weight)? Teachers often resort to images of feathers, breezes, flutes, hummingbirds, and butterflies when confronted by such a singer.

Instead, having experiences in using less mass at greater speeds will help the singer understand the problem quickly. An old adage applies here: "What the student experiences, the student remembers." The singer has not had the experience of being a feather or butterfly, but can experience the tension, or reduction of tension, when using the body efficiently.

You will need another person to help you with the following experiment in balance.

Take a walk around the room, using a normal pace and stride. Be sure to use your normal energy in your stride, or you will sabotage the exercise.[1] Your partner, at random, says "stop."

How did you stop? Did you need an additional step to stop? Did you stop with both feet on the floor? See if you can stand balanced on one leg. Balance on the other leg. Problems?

Have your partner walk and stop when you say "stop." Have your partner try to balance first on one leg, then the other.

Problems?

Return to the exercise. This time the walking person will try to stop on one foot. Be sure to use your normal energy in your stride, or you will sabotage the exercise.

What did you and your partner experience? If you have problems maintaining your balance (most people initially have trouble stopping on one foot), it is probably because your head is not aligned with the rest of your body.

This lack of balance becomes even more pronounced when moving from quicker energized steps to slower ones. Lack of balance is one reason singers tend to rush longer notes when they follow shorter notes, as in this example:

◆ Illustration 4-4 ◆

Perform the rhythm in Illustration 4-4 by running (or using very quick walking steps) for the eighth notes and walking for the others: be careful to balance on one foot, particularly during the half note.

---

[1]Many people shorten their stride (taking baby steps) to avoid losing their balance. You will learn more about your balance by maintaining the normal length and energy of your stride.

Notice what you do to stop your motion after the quicker notes. Notice also that you used more effort to stop for the half note on the end. Maybe you succeeded in stopping by bringing your foot down more forcefully; this was a use of weight. A basic rule in Western music has evolved out of the physical phenomenon you just experienced: following a series of shorter notes, a long note receives extra weight.

PLASTICITY

The way you used your body as you moved between the steps of the exercises is called plasticity. It is the final element of the Dalcroze equation. Plasticity, the quality of the movement between the steps (or pitches), is what gives the performer and audience the affective[2] "feel" of the music. Motion causes emotion, just as emotion causes motion. Smile, and certain chemicals are released in the brain, eventually leading to the affect of "pleasure"; grimace, and the affect of displeasure or pain will follow.

Imagine you are patting a sick puppy. Notice what happens *before* the first pat, *during* the pat, and *between* the pats. Now stroke the puppy as if you were playing with him and say, "Good dog!" Notice what happens *before, between,* and *during* the strokes. Repeat the exercise several times until you understand how your attitude affects your gestures and your gestures affect your attitude.

Also, notice the difference in the space between the gentle ("poor sick puppy") and more exuberant ("good dog") movements. The differences reflect the changes in plasticity (also energy, weight, and direction). Plasticity is the subtle movement that informs the other elements (energy, weight, etc.). How does this apply to a singer? It means not only that taking a breath before a phrase is important, but *how* the breath is taken (the affective reason) is equally important. For example, the breath taken for a scream is different from one taken for a loud sigh.

This has been your brief introduction to the elements of the Dalcroze equation. You will see them again in various forms throughout the remainder of this book, beginning with the way in that space, time, weight, plasticity, energy, and balance are used in what Jaques-Dalcroze called the *normative measure.*

---

[2]*Affect* here means the "conscious, subjective aspect of an emotion" (*Webster's,* p. 19). I use the term to apply to all the physical sensations we label "emotion" or "feeling."

◆ Chapter 5 ◆

the normative measure

and

its effect

This chapter is about the normative measure and its constituent parts: *arrhythm, errhythm,* and *eurhythm.* The term *normative measure* may be considered a synonym for "metrically normal measure." Beats come in various qualities of motion, such as "push, glide, stretch, lift, roll, slide, skip, hop." If the patterns of the qualities are repeated—as in

push gliiide ^{lift} **push** gliiide ^{lift} **push** gliiide ^{lift}

then we experience the sensation of "meter," in this example, a meter in three. The audience comes to expect _{push,} gliiide, ^{lift}, but a good composer will find a way to vary the pattern to ensure the audience keeps paying attention. The composer could write "_{push} ^{lift} gliiide" or "gliiide ^{lift} _{push.}" However, the audience will not understand the changes unless it has the original pattern in mind, or the performer fails to make the changes clear.

The effect of performing the normative measures and variations well are similar to telling funny stories in which language is twisted unexpectedly. Unfortunately, all too often in concerts neither the performers nor the audience understand the punch line. While there are various reasons for the artists' and audiences' lack of understanding, two of the most critical reasons are that (1) neither the performers nor the audiences have been taught what they should expect as they listen to "art" music; (2) the performers of "art" music have not been doing their job.

Understanding the use of the normative measure will provide one solution to the problem of boring performances. To help you understand the normative measure, you need to understand these terms:

Arrhythm

Errhythm

Eurhythm

Jaques-Dalcroze understood and used many of the ancient Greek philosophers' theories of rhythm. Physicians adopted two of the terms for medical purposes: if your doctor listens to your heart, and it is normal, the doctor will write "eurhythmia" on your medical chart. If the doctor writes "arrhythmia," you will probably be taken to the hospital!

ARRHYTHM

We can see arrhythm around us in everyday life. Watch a baby learning to walk or a young child learning to ride a bicycle, and you will see awkward gestures, lack of balance, and a tendency to run into immovable objects. This is arrhythm in action.

Arrhythm shows up in musical studies when performers cannot keep a steady beat, when they inappropriately pounce on high notes while singing lower notes timidly, or when they are physically graceless in their presentation. Arrhythm seems to be a part of the initial learning process whether we are speaking of musical or athletic skills (since both must be learned physically).

ERRHYTHM

What is *errhythm* (pronounced as if the "r" was elongated)? An errhythmic performance is correct, mechanical, and, ultimately, lifeless. Another word for errhythm is "timing." Errhythm is with us everywhere in our artistic lives. We hear errhythmic performances in live concerts, recordings, and, most of all, with our students. In fact, many music teachers (not just voice teachers) hope fervently that their students attain, at least, an errhythmic performance.

How many performances have you heard where all the correct notes, rhythms, words, and, perhaps, even the dynamic markings were followed, yet it somehow seemed dull? Several years ago, a Handel opera festival was presented in New York City. The singers had been coached (and coached and coached) in the proper ornaments and embellishments, cadenzas, trills, and fioraturas, and the costumes and sets were quite elaborate. The singers' voices were, in terms of technique, quite lovely.

But after the first performance, the audience stayed away in droves. Why? Word quickly spread that the productions were boring: they were correct, lifeless, mechanical, and dull. In short, errhythm (timing) had struck again.

EURHYTHM

Eurhythm, introduced earlier, may be defined as the varieties of rhythmic flow through space. Eurhythm is a major component in expressive performance and is the result of the balancing and shifting of the elements in the Dalcroze equation. It is the movement felt by the performer and subconsciously perceived by the audience but is not visible to the audience.

EFFECT OF THE NORMATIVE MEASURE

Jaques-Dalcroze's teachers (Franck, Fauré, Lussy) came from the French tradition of musical performance. The French have always been concerned with the nuances of life, and this concern has influenced the way they perceive music. One result of this concern for nuance (literally, shade or hue) is the feeling that every beat within a measure should have its own quality, and that the composer changes this quality at will. This approach to music making varies quite a bit from the German theorists who base their musical beats on poetic "feet." A result of this Germanic approach is the theory that music has "strong" and "weak" beats. Thus the beats in a 4/4 measure would appear like this:

◆ Illustration 5-1 ◆

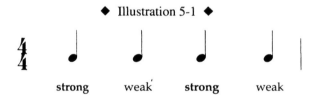

strong weak strong weak

Look familiar? The music theory taught in American schools is based on the German system. But the French, with their Gaelic love of nuance, suggest that metrics should be based not only on literary theories, but also on other inherently expressive qualities. Jaques-Dalcroze used three Greek terms to describe these typical beat qualities: crusic, metacrusic, and anacrusic.

Crusis

"Crusic" comes from the Greek *crusoic* and means "strike."

Imagine you have a baseball bat in your hands. Take a batter's stance and prepare to hit the ball. Swing the bat and imagine making contact with the ball.

The instant of contact is called *crusis*.

Metacrusis

> **Swing again, make contact with the ball, and notice what you do with the bat immediately after contact.**

You probably followed through with the swing and ended with your muscles relaxing as you lowered the bat. The moment of release following the crusis is called *metacrusis*.

Anacrusis

> **Prepare to swing again, this time in slow motion. Be attentive to the way you prepare to hit the ball.**

You probably shifted your weight to your back foot as you pulled the bat back, then shifted it forward as you swung the bat forward. All this preparation is called the *anacrusis*.

> **Swing again, at the normal speed, with the intention of hitting the ball lightly. Swing again, with the intention of hitting a home run.**

Be attentive to the anacrusis, and you might discover that the anacrusis is different for each swing. In fact, the anacrusis informs, or determines, the kind of crusis. In other words, *the type of preparation determines the type of results*.

Consider how this principle applies to our teaching and performing. How can we expect musical results (crusis) if we have unmusical preparation (anacrusis)? How can we expect an expressive performance if we use inexpressive preparation? I have heard of one occasion where a teacher approached her student after the student's public performance and said, "You were stiff and inexpressive. I thought you could do better."

The student was instantly reduced to tears, saying, "But everything was right. I didn't have any memory slips, and I thought I sounded good."

"Yes, that was all right," the teacher continued, "but you didn't *do* anything with the music. I thought you were more expressive than that!"

The student had been led to believe that singing the correct notes, words, and rhythms with a good technique was enough. Whereas her teacher assumed the singer would "throw in" whatever it took to be expressive. *The problem was that the teacher did not teach expressiveness as part of the learning process but still expected the student to perform expressively.* All of us, whether teacher or performer, occasionally spend more time developing the technical ability to perform certain literature. There is certainly nothing wrong in using this approach occasionally, but to do so all the time, with every composition, dulls our emotive abilities. Therein lies the danger: our technical skills flourish while our expressive skills languish.

Stretching Metacrusis

By performing the preceding exercises, you have experienced the sensation of crusis, metacrusis, and anacrusis. Another type of quality occurs in 4/4 on beat 3, which is the feeling of a stretching metacrusis.

> **Go back to your imaginary bat and pretend you are at batting practice. Hit the ball and immediately prepare to swing at another pitch. Ready? Go.**

The movement that begins after the follow-through (metacrusis) and stretches to the beginning of the anacrusis is the stretching metacrusis. Where does the anacrusis begin? There are several possibilities, but let's assume it begins the moment you shift your weight, and the bat, away from the incoming ball.

> **Practice the entire set, crusis, metacrusis, stretching metacrusis, anacrusis, again as you swing your imaginary bat.**

Now place the crusi into the musical setting of the normative measure by performing the following exercise.

1. While standing, extend your left arm in front of you. Then push it toward the floor as you say "push." Be sure the energy in your voice matches the gesture as you do it. Try it again. Try it with your right arm. Try it with both arms.

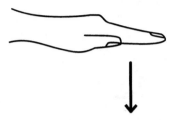

2. Move your left arm, palm down, across the front of your body and say "glide." Enjoy the sound and feeling of the *gl* of "glide." Try it again. Try it with your right arm. Try it with both arms (your arms should cross in front of you).

3. Beginning in the center of your body, with your left arm still extended, move it to your left as you say "stretch." Try it again. Try it with your right arm. Try it with both arms.

4. Finally, starting from the end of "stretch," lift your arm as you say "lift."

As you repeat the entire pattern, you should have something similar to this:

◆ Illustration 5-2 ◆

Right arm pattern

"Pusssh"

"Stretch"

"Glide"

"Lift"

(The left arm pattern is the reverse.)

After you are comfortable with the pattern (you probably recognize it as the traditional 4/4 conducting pattern), change the words: "push" becomes "crusis," "glide" becomes "metacrusis," "stretch" remains "stretch" ("stretching metacrusis" becomes difficult to say at quicker tempos), and "lift" becomes "anacrusis."

There you have the pattern for the normative measure in 4/4. In 3/4, it appears as follows:

◆ Illustration 5-3 ◆

Right arm pattern

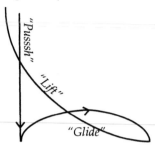

(The left arm pattern is the reverse.)

In 2/4, it appears as follows:

◆ Illustration 5-4 ◆

Right arm pattern

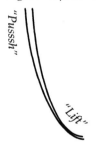

(The left arm pattern is the reverse.)

If the qualities of beats in a normative measure were drawn, they might look like this:

◆ Illustration 5-5 ◆

Crusis Metacrusis *STRETCHING METACRUSIS* ANACRUSIS

Compare this to the "German" measure and you can see they would sound quite different:

strong   weak   strong   weak

You can also see the many possibilities for variety that the normative measure provides, since the various crusi may be switched around to create different types of movement within measures. For example, if all beats have equal duration, we would find what we used in Illustration 5-5:

But if the composer divided any of the beats (subdivision), we would perform them as in Illustration 5-6:

◆ **Illustration 5-6** ◆

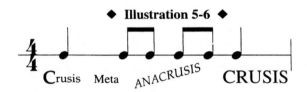

If you are puzzled by the differences, move around the room in this manner:

step run run run run step

Why was the fourth beat of the measure so heavy? If you really moved quickly on the "run, run, run, run," then you had to put on the brakes hard in order to stop. A rule of subdivision might be stated as follows: the more a beat is subdivided, the more anacrusic it becomes; the beat following an anacrusic pattern receives more weight. If you performed the preceding exercise, you discovered the rule is based on physical principles. By using diacritical markings (e.g., *sfz, subito piano*) the composer may indicate unusual effects within a measure (Beethoven did this continually—but again, he assumed the performer and audience knew what rule he was breaking).

But how does the performer and the audience experience and study these agogic twists and turnings? Through movement which has been internalized. When I am asked, as a Dalcroze teacher, why I insist on using movement to teach music, my response is, "Because you have to. Of the three elements of music (pitch, dynamics, rhythm), two of them, dynamics and rhythm, come through motion. Performers cannot perform well unless they have a strong internal kinesthetic sense of the music."

◆ Chapter 6 ◆

understanding music through kinesthetics

Jaques-Dalcroze arrived at the core of his methodology when he developed the use of rhythmic movement (rhythmics) for the teaching of music. It was also the source of some of his harshest criticism from academic music teachers.[1]

He realized that people experience emotions with their bodies through muscular contractions and releases. Emotions are felt by everyone and understood by no one, particularly the person experiencing them. Philosophers through the ages have tried to understand emotions by finding their "seat" or root. The ancient Jews believed they resided in the liver or kidneys. By the time of the Western Renaissance, emotions were thought to be located in the heart: our literature and common speech (as in "I love you with all my heart") still alludes to this seat of feeling.

The theories of twentieth-century psychologists range from speculating that feelings are complex chemical reactions to viewing them as entirely nonexistent. A majority, however, seem to agree that something does happen in our bodies when we experience emotions. The arguments now are about which comes first: the affect that triggers the physical reaction or the physical reaction being perceived as affect.

Evidence is accumulating that "there are . . . extensive neural connections in the brain from those parts that oversee movement, equilibrium, and balance of the body to those parts that direct thought and emo-

[1]The criticism was not based strictly on academic concerns. Jaques-Dalcroze had his students perform movement training in clothing that was considered skimpy at the time. He nearly lost his lease once because the conservatory board, his "landlord," objected to the bare arms and legs of the young ladies. Mrs. Jaques-Dalcroze asked the all-male board if they did not like young ladies' arms and legs, which, of course, they did. After some deliberation and harumphing, the lease was renewed.

tion . . . the two [brain and body] are in an indissoluble union. The implication is that we literally think with our bodies, that is, we think kinesically" (Seitz, p. 52). So movement and physical positioning can create affect, and vice versa. Raise your shoulders, make your breathing quick and shallow, widen your eyes, drop your jaw, and you will probably discover a feeling of panic or terror: this is affect reacting to physical signals.

AFFECT AND MOVEMENT

Reproduce the vocal sounds you make when crying, allowing your face and body to move as if you were crying. Soon you will probably be thinking sad thoughts and possibly shedding tears. Again, this is affect responding to your body that responded to your thoughts (when you read the directions and consciously recreated your physical reaction).

Use the following exercises, or games, to explore the affect of movement on emotion:

> **Draw curving lines in the air with one hand. Increase and decrease the energy you use as you draw the curves. Add a vocal sound that follows what you draw and match the energy of your drawn lines with your vocal energy. Alternate your arms to avoid tiredness.**

Did your thoughts and feelings change as you performed this exercise? If you do not know, try the exercise again and pay attention to what you are thinking and the emotional shading of your thoughts.

> **Change the type of lines you are drawing, perhaps making them straight or angular, and notice the effect, if any, of the drawing on the quality of your vocal sound.**

> **Change the procedure, and make a vocal sound first, then draw it in the air. Try making the sound continuous, changing the quality of the sound as you go. Allow your drawing to change as the sound changes.**

Perhaps you discovered you had difficulty in matching your movements with your voice, or vice versa. Join the crowd. This usually happens when we begin adding our voices to movement because our voices are disconnected from our bodies!

The exercises you have just used are even more interesting when somebody else draws your vocal sounds and your draw theirs. Remember, you are not singing a "song" but rather simply wordless vocal sounds.

I mentioned in the first paragraph of this chapter that the academic powers that be in Jaques-Dalcroze's time were critical of this newfangled eurhythmic stuff. To them, eurhythmics simply looked like dancing around a room, whereas to study music you had to be at your instrument or standing still. Jaques-Dalcroze disagreed.

Any instrument is soundless until a person pushes the keys, presses a button, or takes a breath. So, Jaques-Dalcroze reasoned, the first instrument to be trained is the body. The body is capable of making a gesture for any musical sound, and the body is capable of transforming gestures into sound. All the elements of music—melodic shape, rhythm, phrasing, harmony, you name it—can be translated into physical movement. Before pushing the keys or taking a breath to begin singing, it is possible to learn the choreography of a composition.

THE DANCE OF AFFECT

"So?" you might ask. "Let's say you learn the 'dance' of a composition. Where does that lead?" "Well," I reply enigmatically, "let's try something."

Think of a phrase from a favorite song, something musically and technically simple. Sing it aloud. Turn on a tape recorder and record it as you sing. This recording of your initial performance might prove interesting later. Stop the recorder after your performance.

1. Sing the phrase in your head, drawing the melodic outline in the air with either hand.

2. With the other hand, draw the "feeling" of the phrase as you sing it in your head. How do you "draw a feeling"? Make a fist and shake it in the air. Allow your face to show how your fist feels. What emotion did you feel?

3. Repeat step 1 while shaking your fist and scrunching your face. Notice any difference in the quality of the gesture in your "phrase" hand?

4. Sing the phrase aloud while drawing it.

5. Allow your "feeling" hand to show the "feeling" of the phrase as you sing it.

6. Sing the phrase with both hands performing their tasks.

7. Finally, sing the phrase with one hand performing both tasks, drawing the melodic outline with "feeling." Record your final performance and compare it with your initial performance.

What did you discover as you went through these steps? Ideally, you began to experience the effect of affect and motion on your performance. If you recorded your performances, listen for differences, that's all, just differences. Try not to evaluate one as better or worse than the other, at least not yet. Many people immediately want to make a judgment about whether something is good or bad. Later, I discuss the effects of judgmental thinking in the chapter on improvisation.

The outcome of the preceding experiment is one answer to the question of why learning the dance of a piece is important. Ideally, you experienced a change in your emotions as you changed the movements, and your voice followed suit.

The same exercise works with new pieces: you can understand them without having to sing through them. Most of us, though, myself included, can hardly wait to sing through a new piece. Why? To get a feel for the piece! The problem with singing through it is that we become distracted by sound, or technical demands, and forget to listen to the music! A goal of Dalcroze teaching is sight-reading that is as musically expressive as possible, so expression is part of the learning process from the beginning. The all-too-typical learning process deals with everything *but* expression until the dress rehearsal.

PLAYING DETECTIVE

Imagine picking up a new piece that looks interesting, and playing detective. "O.K., it's by Arnold Jones, in English. Twentieth century? Look's tonal. It's in 3/4, maybe some kind of waltz. G major. Is it from an opera? No. The text is about dancing . . . in the moonlight. The melody goes up and down; up, up, fermata on "boa." Who's singing this? Hold on, what are these accidentals doing here? A D-sharp in G major? Rhythm has changed. Words about "jumping over fences, chasing the dog," B minor, slower tempo. Back to G major, quicker tempo . . . "the party goes on" . . . ka-boom. End of piece." Meanwhile, you have been using your arms and body to illustrate what you see, all the tempo changes, phrasing, dynamics, and so on.

The internal dialogue just described is the type of detective work that, over time, can be done almost instantly when looking at a new piece (the gestures will all eventually be internalized: felt, but not necessarily seen). Notice it was unnecessary to sing through it, yet you can gain a sense of the musical and dramatic intent of the composer that you might not have if you were concerned about correct rhythms, melody, and technique.

The score becomes a picture of the movements of sound through space. It tells us where to glide, float, move quickly, slowly, accelerate, or slow down. We constantly question, "Why jump here and glide there? What affect am I depicting by turning these gestures into sound?"

Excellent sight-readers who read musically—not sight-readers who simply get the notes—go through this type of internal dialogue and internalized movement instantly as they read. There are very few sight-readers of this caliber, but most of us can learn to read more expressively.

SKILLS FOR EXPRESSIVE READING

Although there are several skills that come into play during expressive reading, three are paramount among the skills:

1. organizing melodic patterns,
2. organizing metric patterns,
3. organizing the text into coherent meanings.

An attitude of improvisatory risk taking, instead of having to "get everything right," accompanies these skills. What about technical demands? Will sight-readers hurt themselves if they read with a sense of abandon? No. The assumption behind this question is that our bodies do not function well without conscious control and will lurch into walls unless controlled by our cognition. I have never found this to be true because our bodies have built-in defense mechanisms that we override at our risk. What is the feared vocal "crack," that phenomenon which besets so many young—and not so young—male singers? It is simply the vocal muscles protecting themselves from too much tension.

On the contrary, physical injuries happen when we try too hard, when our cognition overrides our physical defense responses. Barry Green in *The Inner Game of Music* and Timothy Gallwey in *The Inner Game of Tennis* address this issue nicely. The field of arts medicine exists primarily because of the neurotic tendency to override the body's good sense.

Besides trying to make the body work, most of us have a physical equation we carry around with us: "concentration = tension." Ask most singers to perform a section of an aria (this induces "concentration") and they usually place tension in various parts of their bodies. You might see shoulders raise, arms and hands stiffen, eyebrows raise, jaws tighten, knees straighten. You will hopefully not see all these symptoms in one singer; if you do, that singer is in serious trouble.

Certain types of tension are so associated with certain voice types that Boris Goldovsky has named them. For example, a bent arm that is pulled back and slightly away from the body, usually with a flexed wrist so the palm is almost perpendicular with the floor is called "soprano elbow" or "soprano wrist." Raising the body up slightly, as if balancing on the balls of the feet, is called "tenor toes."

Teachers of the Alexander technique speak of "debauched sensibilities," that is, tension which we have grown so accustomed to that it seems natural. A female student who once studied with me kept so much tension in her shoulders that they were parallel to the floor. The trapezius muscles which held them up were so tight that they felt more like bones than muscle. In fact, she maintained they *were* bones! You can imagine the tension that was present in her movement and her singing.

The concentration = tension equation and debauched sensibilities in which tension is perceived as natural are two powerful forces that militate against expressive performance. How can one move gracefully with elegant curves (as Debussy's music often moves) when living in an Anton Webern body?

◆ Chapter 7 ◆

improvisation

In a delightfully sardonic essay titled "The Young Lady of the Conservatory," (Jaques-Dalcroze, *Rhythm, Music & Education*, p. 61) Jaques-Dalcroze had an imaginary conversation with the father of a conservatory student. When Jaques-Dalcroze asked the father what pieces his daughter played at home for family entertainment, the reply was that she didn't because she was always "between pieces," meaning she could not remember pieces she had recently performed nor would she perform the pieces she was presently learning.

Jaques-Dalcroze asked what kind of music the daughter "made up" when she simply sat at the piano and expressed her feelings of the moment. The father replied that she did not do such a thing because she could only play what someone else had written.

Sound familiar? Do you ever begin singing to express your feelings, making up the music and text as you go? Have you ever wanted to sing for your friends or family to express your feelings, but could not think of a piece you would be able to remember completely, so you didn't? What prevents us from simply making musical sounds and improvising texts that express our feelings? The answers we give are typically these:

- ◆ I feel silly.
- ◆ I can't make up words that are logical, or rhyme, or don't simply sound dumb!
- ◆ I can't make up a melody.
- ◆ I can't make up rhythms.
- ◆ I can't, I can't, I can't!

Most performers have become spectators to making music. We have been conditioned to be reactive to the feelings, organizing systems, and perceptions of the composers, all of which are represented in the score, and we seldom share in the creation of the music. Jaques-Dalcroze maintained that improvising was the most cogent method a performer could use to discover what is understood about the music being studied. Improvising helps us "own" the music.

PROACTION AND REACTION

Humanist psychologists during the 1960s used the terms *proactive* and *reactive* to describe the way people respond to the environments and challenges that confront them in everyday living. People who habitually react feel helpless and out of control, whereas people who proact generally usually feel empowered and exhilarated. I asserted that we, as performers, have been conditioned to be reactive to the musical score.

Reactive performing says I can only recreate music, I cannot generate it from within myself; I am not capable of making music without a score. Proactive performing says I can create music from within myself.

Reactive performing says, "I have to get louder or softer, faster or slower, because the score (composer) says so." Proactive performing says, "The composer wishes me to get louder or softer, faster or slower, but I will choose how loud/soft, fast/slow to perform."

A reactive attitude says, "The score (composer) controls me." A proactive attitude says, "I control the score and am responsible for making performance decisions."

A reactive student says, "I have to do this because my teacher says so." The proactive student says, "I am following my teacher's suggestion to learn something I don't know."

If a student has difficulties in learning or performance, the reactive teacher experiences this as a negative reflection on the teacher and often responds with frustration; the proactive teacher experiences the same situation as a valuable test for discovering what the teacher now needs to teach and what the student still needs to learn.

IMPROVISATION

Improvisation is a skill that encourages proactivity. The Dalcroze methodology combines kinesthetic training with improvisation to teach us to do the following:

◆ Use all our faculties when learning
◆ Explore movements with our bodies

◆ Use our imagination and creativity

◆ Become aware of the space around us

◆ Become flexible and agile and develop coordination and motor abilities

◆ Develop a complete sense of body awareness

◆ Express feelings through body movement and sound

◆ Develop listening capacity

◆ Use our minds to control our bodies

◆ Develop our abilities to concentrate and pay attention

◆ Feel relaxed while simultaneously having a positive and constructive outlet for physical energy

Improvisatory skill has other positive side effects as well.

Improvisatory Skills Can Reduce Performance Anxiety

As my students develop their improvisatory skills, many of them have reported experiencing an increased sense of confidence. They have discovered specifically that the fear of forgetting, which seems to be a major source of performance anxiety, is reduced. Several have said, "I figure if I forget the words, or melody, or whatever, I can make them up until I remember where I am."

Improvisation Can Aid in Score Study and Understanding Styles

Improvisation can help the performer understand a composer's decisions, which are reflected in the score, by making other decisions through change and contrast. In addition, the best reason for developing improvisational skills is the ability to make one's own music: understanding the style of a composer through improvising makes it the performer's style as well. Jaques-Dalcroze maintained that improvisation is a very sophisticated level of musical accomplishment because it shows all the musical information that has been internalized.

Putting on the style of a composer, like putting on new clothes, does not mean I give up my uniqueness, but rather expands the way I move through the music. "This composer's style is a little snug at my waist; the pant length is good, but it's a little tight in the seat, so I'll have to be careful when I stoop or sit down." The result is that I will understand Mozart's *andante* is different from Beethoven's, which is different from Mahler's.

Mozart moves through E major very differently than Bach, who was different from Mendelssohn, and so on. Improvisation can be a powerful tool in developing this kind of kinesthetic/affective understanding.

It is very difficult, if not impossible, to use kinesthetic training without improvisation, and H. Wesley Balk, former Artistic Director of the Minnesota Opera, is one of the best innovators in improvisatory kinesthetic training working today. He outlines much of his thinking in his books, *Training the Complete Singer/Actor* and *Performance Power*. His videotape, entitled *Opera Without Elephants*, is a wonderful and entertaining summary of his methodology. Many of the following exercises that follow are a result of my contact with him.

Often, in one-to-one teaching situations, the following exercises seem threatening, so, if possible, try them in small groups. However, the exercises can be easily adapted for personal use or one-to-one settings.

THREE EXERCISES IN PLASTICITY

Start by standing in a circle. Begin by modeling the activity.

◆ 1 ◆

Imagine you have a small ball of energy in the palm of your hand. Using your other hand, begin manipulating the ball of energy: stretching, bending, twisting, flattening, throwing—anything that comes into your imagination. Pass the ball of energy to someone else, indicating that the other person should find ways to manipulate it. Continue until everyone has had an opportunity to play with the ball.

On your next turn, play with the ball again, this time adding sound that s t r e t c h e s, b_{ounce}s, t^{hrow}s, $t_w i^s$ts, FLATTENS, and so on. Be sure to vary the quality of your sound and keep it full of energy. Pass the ball around the circle.

On your next turn, rub the energy over an arm, or face, or shoulder, or leg, and have that body part energized while the rest of your body is quiet. Be sure to use different vocal sounds as you perform this exercise. Pass the ball around the circle.

On your next turn, begin moving through space (perhaps from your side of the circle to the other side) using your body to imitate the unusual sounds you are making; be sure your movements match the sounds. Wesley Balk calls this form of exercise "sound in motion." You might walk, crawl, slither, back up, run, use any movement that explores movements you and the group are not accustomed to using. When you reach the person who stands opposite you, it is that person's turn. You might have to remind the person to use sounds as well as gestures.

What to Watch and Listen For
During the Exercise

Most people use smaller and smaller amounts of physical and vocal energy as they try new activities. You will probably have to remind them to keep using their voices and to keep the sound alive.

You will also discover people tend to keep using the same sounds and gestures, so encourage them to vary them. Of course, that means you, the teacher, will have to be willing to constantly vary sounds and gestures.

People will often try to pass the energy quickly because they are self-conscious; encourage them to spend more time playing.

Occasionally a person will stop both sound and action while he or she tries to figure out what to do. Do not allow that, but rather insist that he or she proceed.

Implications of the Exercise

◆ Gestures can become sounds, and sounds can become gestures.

◆ A performer does not stop during a performance when trouble occurs, but finds a way to keep going.

The exercise teaches how to keep voices and bodies energized when trying out new tasks. When sight-reading, peoples' voices are usually weak and their bodies are stiff because they lose their energy when struggling with a new task. The exercise also teaches people that they can keep themselves energized when approaching new tasks.

 ◆ 2 ◆

Once the group has turned on their collective imagination, they are ready to move to the sound of your singing and playing. (This means you must be able to use your voice energetically while not necessarily singing a particular piece.) After you have made sounds for them to move to, call on someone else to be the sound maker. Continue until everyone has had a turn.

What to Watch and Listen For
During the Exercise

Like Exercise 1, the energy in sounds and movements will often diminish unless you remind them to keep them alive. Also, people often resort to repeating the same sounds and gestures. Encourage them to vary them.

Are the people really listening to the sounds? Do their gestures have the same energy as the sounds they are modeling? Usually they do not, and you will have to call this to their attention.

Implications of the Exercise

◆ Everyone can assume leadership responsibilities.

◆ Matching sounds and gestures is possible and important.

◆ Exploring many kinds of sounds and gestures creates possibilities for use in song literature, since music can be beautiful, ugly, or harsh. The premise that "all singing must be beautiful" is insupportable and limits artistic expression.

◆ 3 ◆

> The next step in this process is having the group move to a composition. Ideally you will provide the music by singing as they move, being sure to vary the plasticity, dynamics, and articulation of your performance. You may use a recorded performance if you prefer, but finding one that uses varying qualities of plasticity, dynamics, and articulations can prove difficult. By all means, do not allow the group to hallucinate changes when they do not occur in the recording; encourage them to show you what they actually hear, not what they think or want to hear.
>
> Have the group draw the kinds of beats they hear with their arms as they use their bodies to show the qualities of phrasing and dynamics.

Exercise 3 is also useful in studying a piece of music by showing the quality of beats and meters (is the performer clear about the meter so the listener can sort it out?). Phrasing may be studied by walking in one direction, then changing direction to show a new phrase.

What to Watch and Listen For
During the Exercise

Encourage the group to keep their bodies alive while listening and responding; they have been conditioned to allow their bodies (and brains?) to "die" while listening.

How closely do the gestures and energy match the music? For example, if the music becomes angular, do the gestures become angular?

Implications of the Exercise

We are so conditioned to hallucinating that we often do not hear what is actually occurring. These exercises in plasticity are designed to awaken ears, bodies, and imaginations and then use them to become aware of what actually is happening in the world around us. They also may be used to study music and analyze performances. Having a person sing a composition while the listeners show the meter and quality of beats, dynamics, and phrasing will prove very enlightening to you, the listeners, and the performer, since the listeners will show you what they hear.

MIRROR EXERCISES

The preceding exercises may be adapted to mirror exercises. Mirrors begin with two people facing each other. Person A initiates a slow gesture and Person B imitates as a mirror would (for example, if A moves her right hand, B imitates by moving his left hand). Among other things, the exercise quickly points out any dyslexia!

There are two rules governing mirror exercises: (1) eye contact must be maintained at all times (which may prove very difficult for some people), and (2) gestures must be slow enough to be followed (Person A will tend to move too quickly at first and must be told to slow down).

The rule about eye contact is very important because it forces Person A to both think about what she is doing and observe how another person responds. I have seen many performances where the performer has not achieved that balance and either forgets anyone is listening—the audience quickly senses this and loses interest—or is too concerned about the audience response, leading to anxiety and forgetfulness.

Mirror exercises may also be used to develop concentration and group awareness (if you happen to direct an ensemble). Group awareness is fostered by beginning with two-person mirrors, as just described, then moving to three-person mirrors (one person leading and two following), then four, five, six people as needed (I once had sixty people performing a mirror exercise). Here are some additional uses of mirrors to foster concentration: the leader sings a song while improvising move-ments; the follower sings while following (makes the follower concen-trate like mad!); the two-person mirror sings a canon.

These are the steps for directing the mirror exercise:

---

1. **Form the couples for the mirrors and have each couple decide who will lead and who will follow.**

2. **After the mirrors have begun working, say "Change roles." After several attempts, they should be able to change roles without stopping.**

3. **Next, tell them to change leadership without a command from you and without talking. This is a useful exercise for a singer and accompanist to develop the give and take needed in per-formance.**

   You may now introduce the musical portions described earlier.

EXERCISES THAT DEVELOP ABILITY
TO IMPROVISE TEXT OR MUSIC

Improvising text or music is extremely difficult for many people because of self-imposed rules like these:

- Don't speak or sing until you know what to speak or sing.
- It has to make sense, be logical. These rules make perfect sense in a societal context, but hamstring the artist.

Just as in the plasticity exercises, the gibberish begins without music and then is quickly placed into a musical context. They also work better in a group setting, since they seem threatening in a one-to-one setting.

Teacher says, "When I point to you, start talking and keep talking until I point to someone else."

What to Watch and Listen For
During the Exercise

I have had people literally choke when starting this exercise because they are so concerned about sounding silly or illogical. When that happens, I appoint another person to be teacher and have him point at me and I begin babbling. Some people will respond to the exercise with a gush of words, hardly stopping to take a breath; others will be able to say very little. In both cases, the person will eventually run out of things to say and come to a screeching halt; this is the moment when he or she taps the creative potential. The leader must be patient and allow the person to struggle. Do not allow other people to help (they will feel very uncomfortable during the silence because they are identifying with the person on the hot seat). Such help takes away the opportunity for the person to tap into a new level of personal creativity.

Implications of the Exercise

This exercise begins the exploration of the problem of what happens when a performer forgets the words or music. We are faced with the choice of stopping or continuing on until we know where we are.

EXERCISES IN GIBBERISH

For our purposes, gibberish is the melody and rhythm of another language but not actual words unless it is English gibberish. One goal is to begin to understand language as rhythm, accentuation, articulation, and melody which, together, are perceived as having meaning.

EXERCISES IN GIBBERISH

◆ 1 ◆

Begin with a sound in motion exercise as described in Plasticity Exercise 1. Divide into pairs and use these improvised sounds and motions to converse between partners.

What to Watch and Listen For
During the Exercise

A rule for this exercise is that the person listening cannot interrupt the speaker. This places the burden on the speaker to let the listener know he or she has finished. This is also a way of studying musical phrasing because it raises questions like: How do we know when a phrase is ending? What clues are there in the music?

♦ 2 ♦

> Have the group perform scenes using gibberish. You will proba-
> bly have to provide structure by setting the location and giving
> characters.

What to Watch and Listen For
During the Exercise

Pay close attention to how the group uses rhythm, articulation, accentuation, gestures, and the rise and fall of their voices as they work. These are
elements of language and are useful in the spoken portion of the musical
exercises (Chapter 10).

♦ 3 ♦

> We come to a difficult exercise: English gibberish. You will prob-
> ably have to demonstrate by saying something like " The dog in
> the wall green trash car window, tree scoop feather dust," as if
> you were having a conversation with a friend.

What to Watch and Listen For
During the Exercise

Some people will have problems with this exercise because they want
what they say to be logical. For them, you might assign a nursery poem
that they recite as they converse. See this category in gibberish exercise 2
for further remarks.

MUSICAL GIBBERISH

♦ 1 ♦

> Use a sound in motion exercise to introduce this element. Once
> imaginations are warmed up, have the group converse with musi-
> cal sounds using a non-English gibberish. After they have had
> several experiences with this, introduce English gibberish.

What to Watch and Listen For
During the Exercise

Occasionally people will want to use songs or snippets of songs; encourage them to improvise melodies instead. This exercise can quickly lead to the study of question/answer phrasing that is common in Western music.

◆ **2** ◆

Using a song the group knows well, sing the melody using gibberish for the text.

Change the exercise: use the words but improvise the melody.

Change the exercise: sing the first phrase as written, improvise the music for the second phrase, and continue to alternate phrases in this manner.

Change the exercise: sing the first phrase as written, improvise the words for the second phrase, and continue to alternate.

Change the exercise: sing as written until you say "words!" at which time they improvise the words. When you say "change!" they return to the written words. "Music" means they improvise the music, "change!" they return to the written music.

What to Watch and Listen For
During the Exercise

Same as in Exercise 1.

Implications of the Exercises

These exercises are very useful in understanding style when used in the solo literature with the performer improvising every other phrase in the style of the composer. Ideally, they would eventually lead to an accompanist improvising in different styles at the keyboard and the singer improvising, with text, in the same style. Having the ability to improvise reduces the anxiety caused by the fear of "what will happen if I forget the words?"

◆ Chapter 8 ◆

rhythmic
solfege

We have come to the final element of the Dalcroze methodology: rhythmic solfege. The term refers to the concept that all solfege exercises (such as those found in sight-singing and ear training classes) are performed rhythmically and are always related to scales. Students in rhythmic solfege classes are taught to experience rhythms, intervals, harmonies, and melodies kinesthetically.

This third pillar of the Dalcroze methodology (the other two are rhythmics and improvisation) was adapted from the French system of teaching ear training. I mention the French because of a crucial difference between the French and German-based schools of music theory. First we look at the Fixed Do system and then analyze the differences between the German and French systems of music theory when applied to performance.

FIXED DO SYSTEM

Rhythmic solfege is oriented to the fixed do system. This is the system taught to all European musicians and helps them achieve a very strong sense of relative pitch.

Illustration 8-1 shows the system in its pure form. In this system, the pitch names remain fixed regardless of key, for example, an "A" is always "la." Jaques-Dalcroze combined the fixed do system with numbers to show specific keys: the scale in D major in solfege, for example, would read re, mi, fi, so, la, ti, di, re, and in numbers would read like this:

1, 2, 3, 4, 5, 6, 7, 1

(D, E, F#, G, A, B, C#, D)

◆ Illustration 8-1 ◆

Fixed Do System

do di re ri mi fa fi so si la li ti do

do ti te la le so se fa mi me re ra do

I am often asked if it is necessary to learn solfege if one is already a fluent reader. The answer is no. Most American musicians are trained in the use of letters. Using the English letter names for the pitches is the same as fixed do. However, Americans who wish to communicate with a musician from any other part of the world will discover all other western musicians are trained to use syllables, so learning the syllabic system will facilitate communication.

COMPARISON OF GERMAN AND FRENCH THEORIES

A majority of American musicians have been trained in theory that is based on the German system, and the German system is, in turn, partly based on German literary theory, specifically that which relates to poetic rhythms as I mentioned in Chapter 4.

German theorists have historically shown a fondness for clear-cut definitions, so we have been taught that this interval,

is a perfect fourth, always and forevermore. Amen.

But what if it is placed in the progression of

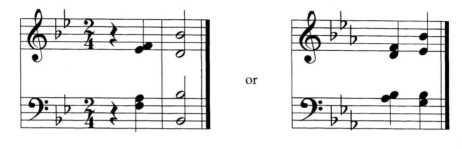

or

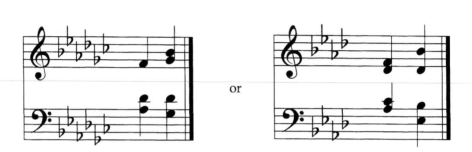

or

Do you feel, and hear, the difference as you move from the F to the B♭ with the changing harmony? Sing the F to the B♭ in all the examples as you play the harmony. Did the sound or feel of your voice change very subtly as you sang them?

Sing them again and this time do not allow your voice to respond to the changing harmonies. What happened? Many singers experience a certain tenseness in the vocal muscles when they do not adjust to changing harmonies. This feeling of tenseness is often mistakenly perceived as a technical problem, but it is an aural problem that can be corrected by understanding where the singer is in the scale and harmony.

German-based theory maintains "A fourth is a fourth!" The French reply, "Perhaps, but fourths come in many flavors." German-based theory also maintains "A pitch is a pitch. You should be able to sing or play it so a machine, such as an oscilloscope, can register it exactly." Again, the French say, "Perhaps. But what color A would you like?"

As you try the following exercise, discover what happens if you allow your voice to adjust to the fluctuating harmonies.

Use a neutral syllable such as "la" to sing the repeated notes at a dynamic of mezzo forte.

◆ **Illustration 8-2** ◆

What did you experience? Many singers report a "shifting" or "changing of the vowel" or some other reaction that seems intuitive. (Singers who experience no change whatsoever are, in my experience, "holding" the pitches rigidly, thus experiencing the "debauched sensibilities" mentioned in Chapter 7. Such debauched sensibilities feel "normal"; however, they prevent the person from being able to respond.) The French suggest that two pitches might be written identically, but sound and feel different because the pitches exist within the framework of scales and rhythms. Jaques-Dalcroze believed this framework was vital to understanding the pieces of scales that we know as "intervals."

Have you ever seen a piece of handiwork produced by creweling? On one side of the crewelwork is the picture or pattern. Turn the material to the back side and you will see how the threads intermingle and crisscross. Jaques-Dalcroze viewed intervals in a similar fashion: intervals are but portions of scales, rather like the picture side of the crewelwork. To perform any interval well, the performer must be aware of the connection between the pitches that form the interval and the scale in which the interval resides.

Sing the following exercise to experience the effect of the internal pitches that determine how the "outside" pitches should be performed.

---

1. Sing only the quarter notes while playing or having someone else perform the unstemmed notes. Pay close attention to any variation in the F's.

2. Sing only the unstemmed notes while playing or having someone else perform the quarter notes.

◆ **Illustration 8-3** ◆

By the way, the irregular spaces between the pitches in this exercise are not due to printer error; rather, I have tried to show the difference in spatial feeling that is felt by expressive performers. This internalized leaning and shifting is what gives the two pitches that form the interval their shading (nuance). Nuance is what creates the music of the intervals. Music is what happens between the pitches.

So far I have explained some of the properties of harmony and movement within intervals. Rhythm has yet another affect. Sing the following exercises to experience the affect of the rhythmic patterns on the scales.

◆ **Exercise 8-1** ◆

do   re   mi fa   so   la   ti   do   ti   la   so fa   mi   re   do

Did you feel/hear the shift in harmony from tonic, to dominant, to tonic? How did the melodic movement feel to you? Smooth? Awkward?

◆ **Exercise 8-2** ◆

do re   mi fa   so   la ti   do ti   la so   fa mi   re   do

What did the rhythmic pattern in 8-2 do to the feeling of the melody?

◆ **Exercise 8-3** ◆

do   re mi   fa   so la   ti   do ti   la   so fa

mi   re do   re   mi fa   so   la ti   do

How did you feel as you sang this example? Was it more, less, or equally comfortable as Exercise 8-2? If it felt different, can you define what the difference was? Notice it is the longest of the three examples. This is because the interplay of the rhythm and scale dictated its length.

Sing Exercises 8-4 and 8-5 together. Provide your own rhythmic accompaniment by clapping or tapping your fingers on a hard surface. Notice the reversal of the rhythmic pattern affects your perception of the movement.

◆ **Exercise 8-4** ◆

do re   mi fa   so la   ti do   ti la   so fa   mi re

do

◆ **Exercise 8-5** ◆

These exercises are in the "simple" key of C major and move step-wise. They can give you some insight into the complex interplay of scales and rhythms. I invite you to compose your own rhythmic formulas to test their effect in other meters.

SUMMARY

This has been a cursory overview of rhythmic solfege. However, this subject is of great importance in the Dalcroze methodology and one that can have an immediate effect on technique. Rhythmic solfege can develop into an extensive study of the interplay of rhythms, scales, and harmonies. The concepts can aid in understanding these principles:

◆ All scales are not alike. G major feels, and sounds, quite different from D major. To the perceptive singer, a leap from the 2nd degree to the 5th degree in F major feels very different than a leap from the 5th up to the 1st degree in C major, even though the pitches (G to C) share the same name.

◆ Position within a scale is important because of shading and weight. This has a direct effect on the technique of the singer as the singer intuitively "shades" his or her voice.

◆ Expressive performance of intervals must include the movement between the pitches of the interval. Feeling the varying space between pitches influences how they are sung.

Take time to review the exercises used in this chapter and invent your own as you explore the affect of rhythm and scales on your technique.

◆ Chapter 9 ◆

the behaviors
for
learning

This chapter looks at the six basic musical behaviors that musicians must possess in order to study and learn efficiently:

1. Paying attention
2. Turning attention to concentration
3. Remembering
4. Reproducing the performance
5. Changing
6. Automating

Jaques-Dalcroze became convinced that successful teaching inculcates musical behaviors in addition to technical skills and literature. He also became aware early in his teaching that his students lacked awareness of their musical and physical environment, and that lack affected their musical behaviors.

"The body, as finely trained as possible, can do only what the brain demands of it. This is true whether the act to be performed is simple or complicated. The aim of [eurhythmics] is stimulation of the imagination, waking up the nervous function, forcing the mind to train the stubborn as well as the cooperative parts of the body" (Spector, p. 145). Arousing the aesthetic awareness of our students is a prime goal for a Dalcrozian.[1] If this sounds too erudite, consider that the opposite of "aesthetic" (awareness of beauty) is "anesthetic!"

---

[1]*Dalcrozian* is a term I use to avoid awkwardness. In this text, Dalcrozian refers to a teacher who uses ideas developed by Dalcroze.

PAYING ATTENTION

The first two problems facing a student have to do with awareness. How often have you had to repeat a direction during a lesson because the student was not paying attention (was unaware)? One way to help a student pay attention is to focus on activities that use the least amount of talking and the most amount of movement and music making. Barry Green in his book *The Inner Game of Music* gives excellent suggestions on "awareness directions" that help the student focus awareness without feeling criticized.

TURNING ATTENTION TO CONCENTRATION

On the heels of attention comes concentration. If a student can pay attention, then concentration is easier. However, the student often needs help to decide what piece of the incoming mass of information to highlight. My students sometimes say that they "just need to concentrate" when they are feeling scattered. When I ask them what they are concentrating on right now, they usually reply that they are "concentrating on concentrating!" Sometimes the student replies, "I'm concentrating on the music." When I ask what part of the music, for example, melody, words, rhythm, or harmony, the student says, "All of it. Everything!" Many students have not learned to extract one part of the musical problem and bring it into their fields of awareness.

Awareness and concentration are issues related to a growing industry: workshops in performance anxieties. Many of the workshops are helpful in providing tips and activities for reduction of tension related to performance nerves, and many focus on providing ways of handling performance stress. But the workshops often have minimal lasting value because they do not address the causes of performance anxiety. I have found that anxiety is generally reduced (1) when we know what we are doing and are able to concentrate on it, and (2) when we concentrate on what we are doing rather than how we are doing. Some people report feeling more relaxed in performances after attending workshops, but only by thinking about something other than what they are performing. In other words, they feel they perform best when becoming unconscious!

Performance anxiety is increased when the singer concentrates on not being nervous or some other negative outcome, such as forgetting the words. Wesley Balk uses a wonderful exercise in his workshops to demonstrate what happens when we concentrate on what we *don't* want to happen. He instructs the students *not* to think about a blue horse. "Don't think of a shining, pale blue horse. . . . with wings." Of course the image grows stronger as the students try to avoid thinking about the image. This exercise points out the importance of paying attention to, and concentrating on, what we *want* to have happen.

REMEMBERING

Many teachers have told me of experiences when a student has struggled with a passage and, finally, sings it well. The teacher, overcome with joy, exclaims, "There! Do that again!" And the student replies, "What?" The student was not paying attention to what she was doing. Remembering what was just done is the first step toward remembering what was done several minutes ago, which, in turn, leads to remembering what was done in last week's lesson, and so on.

Another important aspect of the ability to remember in the context of a lesson is remembering the first performance—the way it was sung at the beginning of lesson—and the final performance (with all the changes). When I ask a new student to reproduce the first performance, which might have included a technical or musical problem, the response is often one of befuddlement: "You want me to sing the mistakes?" The answer is "yes." If the student cannot remember the first performance, then how does the student know what was changed? If you, the teacher, have "fixed" something and the student cannot duplicate the performance, with and without the corrections, you will almost surely have to fix the problem at the next lesson.

REPRODUCING THE PERFORMANCE

The technique of teacher performing and student imitating (called modeling) is a very powerful teaching tool. Whether it is playing, using a gesture to describe the passage, or singing, the teacher's performance should embody all the musical skills available to the teacher, since the teacher's model sets the musical standards for the student's performance.

Reproducing a performance of even several measures is a difficult task for many students. It calls for awareness as well as remembering what was just done and how it was done. A student's first attempts to imitate the teacher's performance are usually crude and self-conscious. You, the teacher, must also be able to exactly replicate your performance several times in order for the student to be able to comprehend what you are doing (yes, the *teacher* has to remember as well as the student). Often, the student will not be able to understand what musical or technical element you are demonstrating, so you might have to exaggerate that element (for example, a diminuendo that becomes extremely quiet).

Teacher modeling can easily be overdone, so it should be used cautiously. Students whose teachers model excessively pick up the teacher's mannerisms and, occasionally, even the teacher's rate of vibrato!

CHANGING

After the student can exactly copy your model performance (ideally you will model several performances so the student can chose the one he or she likes the most), or after the student has worked on a piece for some time, he or she must find ways to change the piece, to begin making it personal. We are witnessing many performances where the singers have wonderful techniques and perform the musically expressive elements such as crescendos or rallentandos correctly (i.e., exactly the way they appear on the page), yet something is missing. As one colleague aptly remarked after hearing such a singer, "The music was coached into him."

A cogent method of making a text personal is to insist that students say it in their own words, particularly if the text is in English. I call this approach "translating." This is a difficult task for many students but very worthwhile, since students discover what they do or do not understand about the text, and you gain insight into their analytical processes.

AUTOMATING

This is the final step that usually happens as the student approaches a performance, and includes all the skills just mentioned. Automation includes the memorization process both of the music and of the exact repetition of the sequence of muscular responses (technique). Once the technical and musical elements of a performance are automated, the student can be attentive to other aspects of performance, like dealing with distractions such as the judges at the competition who talk with each other during the student's performance. However, even when a piece is automated, it is necessary to review the process constantly; we need to automate the behavior, but without becoming automatons.

◆ PART III ◆

Putting the Dalcroze Methodology to Work

You have had a brief overview of the system developed by Emile Jaques-Dalcroze. Consider the implications of rhythmics (use of movement), improvisation, and solfege on how music is taught and performed: physically understanding where we are within the nexus of scale and meter can automatically change our technique. Technique need not be taught separately from the music, but rather as an integrated aspect of meter, scale, and affect.

As mentioned earlier, it seems that we voice teachers often consider technical studies as separate from musicality. Our rationales are actually many variations on a basic theme: we want to "neutralize" the emotional state of the student so the emotions will not "get in the way" of the physical skills we are trying to teach. Jaques-Dalcroze taught that we can be excited *and* in control of our emotions. Yet we often perform as if our emotions will interfere with our production, so the best way to handle them is to avoid them. Don't go near the water until you know how to swim!

As teachers, we are surprised and frustrated with our students when they perform in an emotionless, mechanical way, as if making music were some type of technical study. We call such performances "unmusical." What do we mean? How do we define *musical* or *expressive*? There are many ways to approach learning music in an expressive manner, even in the beginning stages. Gifted teachers and performers have developed and passed along many of the "rules" of expressive performance which are the subject of Chapter 10. However Mathis Lussy and Jaques-Dalcroze were perhaps the first to codify them. In this section, we will look at the "musical rules" and their application.

◆ Chapter 10 ◆

musical rules

INTRODUCTION

We can speculate endlessly about the origins of music, but it probably evolved as an enhancement of language. All languages have inherent rhythms and melodies created by rise and fall of pitch and dynamic emphasis. Native speakers of any language come to understand these rhythms and melodies as having meaning. They can also recognize the meaning of the language even when the rhythm and melody are considerably distorted by a foreign-born speaker. Meaning in a language is created by following the inherent rules of logic for that language. Poets twist and distort these inherent rules to create new meanings and images; humorists often do the same.

The music of a culture follows similar inherent rules that create expectations within the minds of the listeners. Composers assume the audience knows and expects certain outcomes, but compositions that simply fulfill these expectations are usually classified as dull or trite, while compositions which twist and distort these expectations to create new meanings are usually perceived as interesting or exciting.

Mathis Lussy maintained that these rules of Western music could be codified and taught to performers (Lussy, p. iv). However, he did not come to grips with the problem that Dalcroze later attempted to address which is: What do you do if the audience is aesthetically asleep and has no expectations? Or, worse yet, what if the performers are aesthetically asleep and unaware that it is their responsibility to create expectations?

People who are asleep are mindlessly unaware of their surroundings and the universe. We are either aware and "mindful," or asleep and mindless. An aesthetic experience is a mindful experience: our senses, minds, and emotions are all engaged. We celebrate our senses and are entertained; our minds are engaged in seeing ourselves, other people, and our universe in a different way; we sense and understand our shared humanity. An aesthetic experience encompasses *both* mind and emotion.

AESTHETIC CHOICES

It is not my aim to explore aesthetic theories in this book, but we cannot comprehend the full affect of the Dalcroze methodology without some discussion of the outcomes of certain aesthetic choices that were made during the nineteenth and twentieth centuries.

In the nineteenth century, both Lussy and Dalcroze—and other perceptive writers—realized that academicians, performers, and critics were becoming more interested in technique (both instrumental and vocal) for the sake of technique. By the end of the nineteenth century, "higher, faster and louder" seemed to have become the goals of performance.

Singers and teachers of singers jumped on this bandwagon, and by the 1960s we were witnessing "bigger" (louder) voices singing operatic roles that were conceived for smaller (softer) more agile voices. The stories of young, promising singers being pushed into "big-voice" roles are too numerous to list here, but they result from the trend which already existed in the last century.

Composers reacted to the emphasis on technique in several ways. Some used more and more diacritical markings in the scores so the performers had to make fewer and fewer decisions; others declared the entire world of Western musical composition bankrupt and created an entirely different system which was nothing *but* technique. Still others, sharing a similar "music is bankrupt" view, declared music should be about nothing except expressing the composer's feelings, regardless of whether the audience shared, cared for, or even wanted to hear such feelings. True, some composers continued on their creative way, writing music that was appealing for both technical and expressive reasons, but they were the minority.

Meanwhile, where was the audience? Gone . . . to the nearest folk or rock concert. At least there they heard music they simply liked. It made no demands on their intellect and did not have subtle meanings or pretense of artistry, but at least they had composers writing to entertain them and express the emotions, however simplistically, which they (the audience) were feeling. Entertainment and expressing feelings (other than their own) were two elements the so-called serious composers disdained.

Another trend that fosters mindless listening has been dubbed "New Age." On the surface this trend would seem to be the antithesis of rock music, but, as in rock, listeners are invited to sit back and allow the sounds to wash over them. Unlike rock, New Age music has no tension, either harmonically or rhythmically, and is designed to reduce conflict. It is the acoustical version of the worse aspects of the term, *a nice person*: bland, colorless, pleasant, and easily forgettable.

Composers of art music assume the audience is aware of musical conventions, but fewer and fewer listeners know how to listen to music in which, for example, beats are not explicit (as in rock), that does not repeat itself endlessly, and that lasts longer than three minutes (the average length of a "popular" piece). The lack of awareness on the part of the audience presents significant problems for both composer and singer.

TWO ASSUMPTIONS

As I mentioned in Chapter 6, if the performer and audience do not understand the conventions that are being changed by the composer, they will not "get the punch line." Dalcroze methodology stresses the aesthetic experience of music for both the performer *and* listener. "Listen again! Look again! Change!" are directions intended to alert the performer, and ultimately the listener, that something is happening either within the established convention or counter to it. This "alerting" is a rationale for the musical rules that follow. Lussy wrote that the performer needs to search out any "irregularity" within the music and discover ways to highlight the irregularity.

Lussy seems to have based his rules on the following assumptions:

◆ *Expressiveness can be at least partially defined.* Philosophers and scholars have debated the issue of expressiveness and creativity for centuries. While there might not be simple intellectual answers to the question of what constitutes an expressive performance, there are relatively simple answers based on the collective experiences of performers and audiences over several hundred years. Mathis Lussy codified many of these experiences in the nineteenth century and put them into writing.

◆ *Understanding the elements of expression can assist teachers and performers in developing expressive techniques as well as vocal techniques.* Lussy maintained that rules of expression could be codified and taught to performers (Lussy, p. iii). He also wrote that slavishly following the rules would not necessarily create an expressive performer, but that following all the rules will allow a "moderately gifted" performer to "acquire a semblance of artistic feeling" (Lussy, p. iii). Following the rules, or directions of gifted teachers of coaches, will tell the performer what to do and when to do it, but not *why* to do it. Lussy maintained that a truly artistic interpretation was not a series of arbitrary decisions based on whim, but "all is cause and effect, connection and law" (Lussy, p. iv). He also wrote that the rules did not originate with him "for the greatest masters have observed them unconsciously from time immemorial, and artists and people of taste have always submitted to them instinctively" (Lussy, p. iv). He saw his task as one of classifying and formulating them.

A composer of art songs responds to a text, translating feelings into sound, then uses compositional techniques to place these sounds on the page in a code. The musical rules help us to understand that code.

The composer then entrusts the score to the performer and prays the performer knows how to decipher the code. Throughout this code, the composer has sprinkled clues which express the composer's feelings. It is the task of the performer not only to crudely translate the code for the audience, but also to find and translate the expressive clues which inform how the composer felt.

Are performers, then, to slavishly try to express the composer's feelings while setting aside their own? Of course not. By experiencing the composer's perspective, performers have the opportunity to expand and enhance their own affective life. But often performers are unaware of the composer's feelings except in general terms (" 'allegro' is fast, so the composer must be happy"—as a student once said to me). The inability to translate the composer's intentions usually results in performances of the same set of feelings and characterizations over and over, rather like the actor who had roles in thirty different plays in one season but unwittingly used the same characterization thirty times.

There are also performers who "feel" the music and experience great emotional surges during a performance, but are unable to transmit any of this to the audience. It is as if invisible walls separate them from the audience. Their emotional energies are used pushing against the walls, with very little overflowing to the audience. A probable cause for this inability to communicate feelings is the lack of an expressive technique.

Historically, singers have resorted to musical coaches and come away from coaching sessions able to sing the coached literature more expressively. Unfortunately, the coach is usually able to teach the singer the "hows" (what to do), but not the "whys." Lussy and Dalcroze wrote that the rules they formulated were the "whys," the causes and effects of expressive performance. In this book we explore ways in which specific musical tools, taken together, form a technique of expression.

WHAT MAKES A PERFORMANCE EXPRESSIVE?[1]

Before we proceed further into a discussion of expressivity, there is a related area which must be addressed, the area of perception. *Perception*

[1]Many of the concepts in this section are based on the work of Dr. Guy Duckworth, Professor of Music, University of Colorado, Boulder.

is the activity of becoming aware. There are two broad fields of perceptions at work when we talk about performance:

◆ the performer's perceptive field, and
◆ the listener's or audience's perceptive field.

Reactions to a performance are always made from the listener's experience (perceptive field). Composers and performers are always searching for ways to enter the listener's perceptive field. But making the listener pay attention is only half the battle; manipulating the listener's perceptive field is the other half. This is where an expressive technique enters the picture.

What are the attributes of an expressive performance? An expressive performance is:

◆ *Compelling.* The listener is seduced into paying attention and is constantly intrigued and forced to ask, "How what happens?" If the piece is well-known, the listener becomes curious about how the performer will personalize it.

◆ *Clear in musical and emotional intent.* The performer has made decisions about phrasing, structure, and emotional content and is able to communicate them.

◆ *Within the performer's technical and emotional capabilities.* The ability to sing all the pitches does not mean the singer is capable of singing the music. There are seventeen-year-old sopranos capable of singing high B flats, but that does not mean they should attempt to sing *Mi chiamano Mimi*. Singers sometimes lock themselves in vocal knots attempting to perform compositions which are far beyond their technical capabilities. They occasionally miss completely the emotional content of what they are singing. I recently heard a breathy, sixteen-year-old soprano sing Schumann's *Ich grolle nicht*. In addition to being unable to negotiate the wide range of the piece, she could not begin to understand the brooding, dark bitterness of the text since she had never dreamed such emotions could exist.

◆ *Physically congruent.* The performer's face, body, and gestures are congruent with the musical and emotional content. If gestures are used, they enhance and punctuate the emotion being sung. The performer frowns, smiles, laughs, weeps, or grimances, reflecting the emotional content of the composition. The body is free to move as necessary, with shoulders back or slumped, chest raised or sunken, the stance defiant or light, all depending on the emotional content of the piece. The ability to use the face and body precludes the attitude that singers must stand in one fixed position in order to sing well. As the song says, "It ain't necessarily so."

♦ *The performer gives the impression of freshness, spontaneity, and taking risks.* However well rehearsed the performance, it need not become mechanical. Performers in long-running Broadway productions provide good examples of constantly giving the impression of a fresh performance even after hundreds of performances. They accomplish this by finding small things they can do differently such as taking an extra pause, holding a note longer, singing a phrase louder or softer. Taking small risks will help the performer avoid the stigma of a "careful" performance (translation: accurate but dull).

♦ *Appropriate to the style and intentions of the composer.* Many listeners would agree that classically trained singers can sound ludicrous singing pieces from Broadway if they are not aware of the style, just as "pop" singers sound unintentionally funny when attempting to sing classical pieces. Singing in the wrong style sounds just as strange and funny when singing art songs, for example, as when singing a Wolf song with a Schubertian style. The style of any given epoch is a use of space, time, energy, weight, balance, and plasticity—the elements of the Dalcroze equation—which is peculiar to that period. Study of the correspondence and other documents of a period will assist the singer in determining how the elements should be balanced.

The rules are intended to serve as guides instead of edicts, since both Lussy and Dalcroze knew the composer and the performer always have the prerogative to change the rules for expressive purposes. The rules apply to all tonal music from the Baroque until the present. They are dependent on tempo. Slower tempos are usually intended by the composer to use more nuance while quicker tempos use less. Finally, the rules can serve as guides to seeking out expressive clues while learning a score. Finding such clues will help us think and learn more while practicing less.

It is time to explore the actual rules. If you study them diligently, you will begin to analyze a musical score differently because, among other things, you will see how composers use notation to indicate their expressive intentions.

The rules are sprinkled throughout Jaques-Dalcroze's writing so I will not refer to any specific book. They were translated from the original French by Ruth Mueller-Maerlei; I have added further changes in the translations as well as my own comments. I have chosen to use only those which are most often found in song literature.

GENERAL RULES OF PHRASING

◆ PHRASING RULE 1 ◆

When beginning to sing a piece, a breath should be taken on the beat immediately preceding the first note of the melody. In piano playing, this breath needs to be felt as well.

Although this rule seems so obvious that it need not be written, I have noticed students who simply do not breathe before beginning a phrase. Even those who *do* breathe before beginning a phrase tend to take a quick breath that is often out of rhythm, even when the tempo is moderate to slow. Instead of taking a breath that lasts the entire beat (*----- shows the length of the breath), as in Example 1, they breathe as in Example 2.

◆ Example 1 ◆

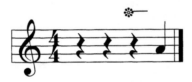

◆ Example 2 ◆

Experience also shows students occasionally do not feel the difference between stopping a breath and taking a breath.

◆ PHRASING RULE 2 ◆

If a phrase contains subphrases, the subphrases need to be separated by either stopping the breath momentarily or by inhaling. The time needed to do so has to be taken from the last note of the (sub)phrase (if there is not a rest) in order to avoid delaying the beginning of the next (sub)phrase.

Here is a short melody by Caccini. The typical singer will have little difficulty with the first phrase, but will probably sing through the shorter phrases if not careful. Remember in this example, and in all the following examples, the (*) indicates either a breath or a sound stop produced by stopping the breath: breathing at every asterisk is not recommended unless the singer enjoys hyperventilating.

◆ *Udite, amanti* by Giulio Caccini ◆

*indicates sound stop

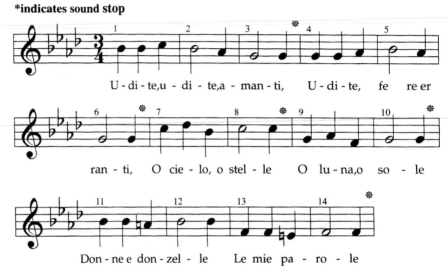

◆ PHRASING RULE 3 ◆

Do not stop the breath in the middle of a rhythmic unit (comparable to breathing in the middle of a word!).

The rhythmic pattern in the Caccini is

Phrasing Rule 3 indicates a breath should not be taken anywhere in the pattern. The rhythmic patterns in the previous example are all bracketed by stopping the sound.

◆ Example 3 ◆

Example 3, presented in an unedited form, illustrates the various rules of phrasing that apply.

◆ PHRASING RULE 4 ◆

When a rhythmic pattern is repeated, breathe or stop the breath before the repetition.

Phrasing Rule 4

◆ PHRASING RULE 5 ◆

Every final note of rhythmic pattern, or phrase, loses some of its sonority (as well as duration) if not followed by a rest. The final note of a crescendo is an exception.

Phrasing Rule 5

measure 2 would be performed

◆ PHRASING RULE 6 ◆

Every group of notes that is not part of a phrase or subphrase but serves to complete the measure (transition, etc.) has to be separated both from the preceding and from the following phrase or subphrase.

◆ PHRASING RULE 7 ◆

In once repeated notes, there must be a break between the two notes if:

a. The two notes are the last and first notes respectively of two consecutive patterns.

b. The two notes are at the beginning of a pattern, period, or phrase. This rule overrides Phrasing Rule 4. If the first note of a rhythmic grouping is repeated, it must be staccato. The second note will have more weight than the first, even if it falls on a metacrusic beat.

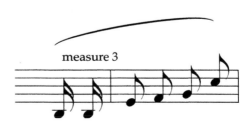

Exceptions:

a. When the two notes represent a weak ending[2] of a rhythm, period, or phrase.

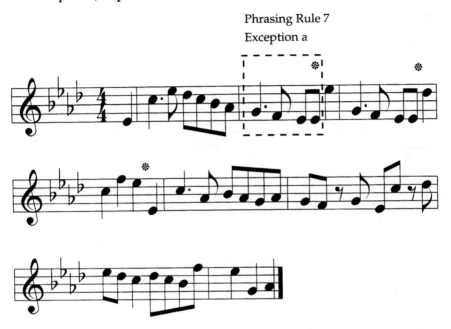

b. When the two notes do not fall under Phrasing Rule 7a or 7b.

[2]I have chosen to use the terms *weak* and *strong* rather than the traditional theoretical terms that have sexist implications: "masculine" (for strong), "feminine" (for weak).

c. **When the two notes are part of a rhythmic formula (e.g., twice as fast).**

◆ PHRASING RULE 8 ◆

An anacrusic pattern should be preceded by a breath. This rule is stronger than Rule 4.

◆ PHRASING RULE 9 ◆

When a series of notes of equal length are followed by a much longer note, breathe after the long note. If this long note is followed by a shorter one to which it resolves (weak ending), breathe after the resolution.

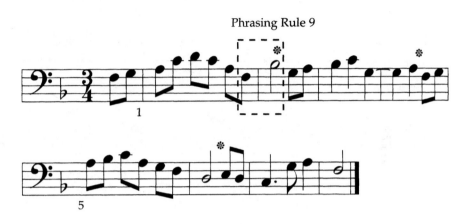

Phrasing Rule 9

◆ PHRASING RULE 10 ◆

The first note of a measure or rhythmic grouping is separated with a breath if the interval to the following note is a fifth or more. Exception: there should be no separation if the two notes constitute a weak ending.

Phrasing Rule 10

◆ PHRASING RULE 11 ◆

Successive group of two notes, each consisting of a long note followed by a shorter one, are separated by lightly stopping the breath.

Phrasing Rule 11

+Refer to Phrasing Rule 6

◆ PHRASING RULE 12 ◆

A breath should nearly always be taken after the (harmonic) "resting" note of a phrase (tonic, dominant, or even subdominant).

Review the musical examples in this section; most of the resting notes coincide with the musical rules.

◆ PHRASING RULE 13 ◆

When a succession of notes of equal value (run, grouppetto) is followed by a longer note, take a breath after this note.

Phrasing Rule 13

◆ PHRASING RULE 14 ◆

When a group of two notes consisting of a short note followed by a longer one is repeated, take a breath before each repetition (compare with Phrasing Rule 12).

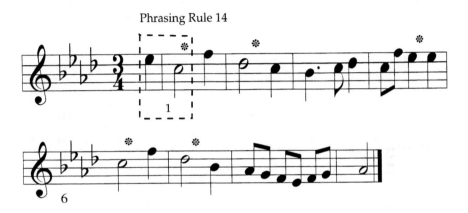

Phrasing Rule 14

RULES OF ACCENTUATION

◆ ACCENTUATION RULE 1 ◆

If the last note of a measure is held over into the next measure, it must be strongly accented (even though it is normally not an accented beat).

Accentuation Rule 1

◆ ACCENTUATION RULE 2 ◆

If a weak beat is subdivided (into eighths, sixteenths, etc.) following a number of undivided beats, the first note of the weak beat must be accented.

Accentuation Rule 2

5

◆ ACCENTUATION RULE 3 ◆

Any note preceded and followed by a rest must be accented, even if it falls on a weak beat.

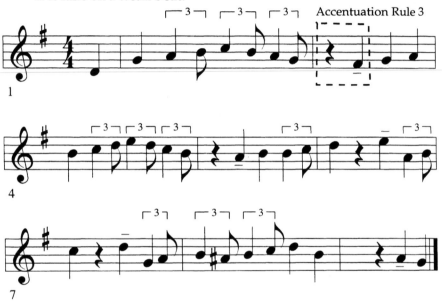

1

4

7

◆ ACCENTUATION RULE 4 ◆

The first note of a measure must be more strongly accented if it has the same pitch as the last note of the preceding measure.

Accentuation Rule 4

1

8

13

For measure 8, refer to Phrasing **Rule 6.**

◆ ACCENTUATION RULE 5 ◆

The highest note of a descending passage must be accented even if it falls on a weak beat.

Refer to Example 1.

◆ ACCENTUATION RULE 6 ◆

Any altered neighbor note or appoggiature must be slightly accented, even on a weak beat. The accent is stronger if it is an upper neighbor note.

Accentuation Rule 6

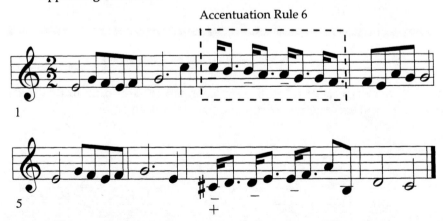

+ These lower neighbors would receive less stress than the upper neighbors.

◆ ACCENTUATION RULE 7 ◆

An altered note that induces modulation must be accented, even on a weak beat.

◆ ACCENTUATION RULE 8 ◆

In a leap of a fourth or greater, either ascending or descending, the second note of the interval receives an accent.

RULES OF NUANCE

◆ NUANCE RULE 1 DYNAMICS ◆

a. Ascending melodies generally ought to be performed with a crescendo (for exception, see Nuance Rule 12b).

b. Descending melodies generally ought to be performed with a diminuendo (for exception, see Rule 12a).

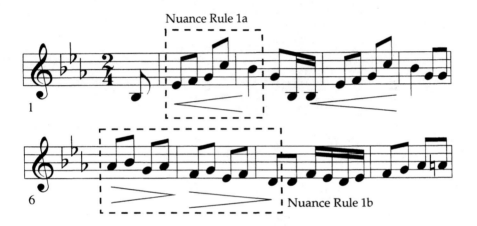

◆ NUANCE RULE 2 ◆

The notes of a melody are not all of equal importance and thus require different amounts of intensity. Very active, fast passages require less dynamic differentiation; slow passages with notes of equal value need more.

The quicker the tempo, the less the shading.

◆ NUANCE RULE 3 ◆

A long note in an ascending run participates in the general crescendo by increasing its intensity. However, if this long note is the last one of the run, it must end in a diminuendo.

Nuance Rule 3

◆ NUANCE RULE 4 ◆

Repeated notes of the same pitch receive a crescendo.

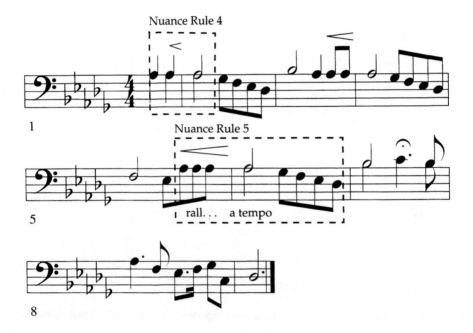

◆ NUANCE RULE 5 ◆

Repeated notes leading to the return of the melody are performed with a crescendo and a rallentando.

◆ NUANCE RULE 6 ◆

If a musical entity (motif, phrase, section, etc.) is repeated immediately, it must be separated (by breathing or articulation) and performed with different dynamics (forte becomes piano, and vice versa).

◆ NUANCE RULE 7 ◆

The transition to the return of the melody receives a rallentando (see Nuance Rule 5).

◆ NUANCE RULE 8 ◆

a. A series of stepwise moving notes of equal value at the end of a melody are to be performed staccato.

b. If this series leads to the return of the melody, a rallentando is also required (see Nuance Rules 5 and 7).

Nuance Rule 8a and 8b

◆ NUANCE RULE 9 ◆

If the first notes of a melody are twice as long or longer than the notes of the run leading to its return, the run should get a rallentando that doubles the value of its last notes.

Nuance Rule 10.N.B.:
The rallentando applies
to the rests, not the
chords (or single notes).

◆ NUANCE RULE 10 ◆

Rests between the final single notes (chords) of a piece are to be performed with a rallentando.

◆ NUANCE RULE 11 ◆

A series of notes of equal value in an otherwise rhythmically varied piece should be strongly accented.

◆ NUANCE RULE 12 ◆

a. **When a descending melody leads to the return of a forte or fortissimo theme, it must be performed with a crescendo.**

b. **When an ascending melody leads to the return of a piano or pianissimo theme, it must be performed with a diminuendo (exception to Nuance Rule 1a).**

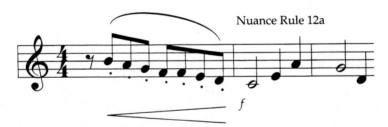

Nuance Rule 12a

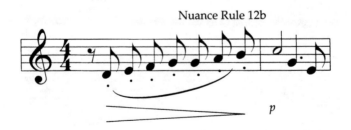

Nuance Rule 12b

◆ NUANCE RULE 13 ◆

The first of two slurred notes of equal value is always performed stronger (more accented, more weight) than the second one, even if the second note falls on a strong beat.

Thus even the banal little composition used for Example 3, although appearing quite simple, takes on a new level of complexity when the rules are added:

Moderato

Writing the musical effects of the rules begins to make the score appear very complicated, so I am not suggesting you write the effects into the score. My goal is that you begin to hear what makes a performance expressive (or, more typically, inexpressive) and be able to give concrete reasons.

◆ Chapter 11 ◆

applying eurhythmics

to

technique

This chapter addresses the following areas:

◆ Performer controls

◆ Voice classification

◆ Breathing

◆ Articulation

◆ Coordinating ear and voice

◆ Coordinating ear and body

◆ Affect and its effect on technique

◆ Three methods of processing information

◆ Three forms of kinesthesia

Although I have written a good deal so far about the importance of balancing technical studies with musical studies, do not interpret this focus as a lack of interest in technique. If a person wishes to study singing seriously, then technical studies cannot be avoided unless the student has one of those one-in-a-million voices where the muscles, ear, and mind are completely coordinated, in short, a real "natural talent." Even then, naturally talented singers should understand as much as possible about their personal technique because as they age or sing under less than ideal conditions, they will experience vocal changes and occasional difficulties. Understanding how they do what they do will assist them in working through troublesome times.

The recurring issue of this book is not one of physical technique versus expressive technique, but rather how to develop both. I used to believe that 90 percent of performing was mental and the remainder was physical. However over a period of several years, I came to understand that we think with our bodies through movement. When we begin to "think" physically about expression as well as "technique," we begin to meld the two seemingly different approaches until they are inseparable.

In correcting musical or technical problems either for myself or my students, it is my experience that a majority of the problems I encounter are musical, rather than "technical," and often fall into three broad categories.

1. Rhythm. More often than not, rhythmic difficulties are associated with lack of physical coordination. Here are some examples of poor coordination:

♦ Difficulty maintaining a steady beat

♦ Inability to perform subdivisions and dotted patterns correctly even though the mathematics of the subdivisions ($\eighthnote\,\eighthnote = \quarternote$) are understood

♦ Inability to vary the quality of the beats, resulting in performances in which everything sounds the same

2. Faulty Aural Perceptions. Ill-formed aural "images"(which I call the "vocal images") are the result of listening primarily to pop singers and attempting to imitate them, or not listening to classical singers enough to know what voices are capable of. Lack of listening to art music continues to be a major problem in training singers; an increasing number of voice students enter our studios with no aural goals in mind other than singing "better."[1]

3. Lack of Awareness of Harmony and/or Structure. Singing without understanding of phrasing results in poor choices of where to breathe. Singing without awareness of harmony leads to intonation difficulties and vocal tension, even when all the other elements of good physical technique are present (registration, vowel modification, etc.).

The more we know about physiology and acoustics and their manipulation, the better our technique will be. There are several fine books available that delve into technique. Each book has its supporters and detractors, but every singer and teacher should have them in a personal library because they are valuable resources.[2] However, well done as these books are, they do not delve into musical considerations (except for Volume 2 of the Garcia), whereas my thesis here is that *developing musical*

---

[1]This attitude is analogous to a traveler beginning a journey without a specific destination, but rather with the intention of "going somewhere."

[2]See Doscher, Miller, Vennard, Fields, Garcia, Foote, and Coffin.

understanding will inform and improve technique. As voice teachers, most of us have been trained to develop technique, but few of us have been trained to teach musical understanding.

I have also chosen to avoid discussing specific vocal techniques I use because (1) the books just mentioned, as well as others, cover that territory quite well, and (2) it seems that voice teachers can agree on very little. Also, I do not wish to distract from my central message: you can enhance musical performance regardless of your technical approach.

Part of my avoidance of presenting my personal technique springs from an experience I once had at a symposium of twenty-five voice teachers convened by an otolaryngologist. His goal for the session was to attempt to make physiological sense of what voice teachers mean by the various terms we use. His first question of the day was, What do you mean by the term *support*? Three and a half hours later, with glazed eyes, he stopped the discussion by saying that obviously none of us could even agree on what he thought was a basic concept for teachers.

I will discuss several general topics related to basic technical issues but from my experience as a eurhythmics teacher as well as a voice teacher. I maintain that instilling musical behaviors and understanding should occur in all phases of the lesson, and that even standard technical exercises can be musical. You are capable of creating music even during your warm-ups. The exercises are those I use with beginning singers and, with adaptations, advanced singers as well.

PERFORMER CONTROLS

The term performer controls[3] refers to the aspects of music that are under the direct control of the performer: tempo, dynamics, and articulation. All other musical elements are indicated by the composer, that is, scales, harmonies, durations. This is true of all Western music.

Composers indicate tempos and dynamics when they write "allegro" and "forte," but how fast is the allegro, and what is its relationship to other tempos? How loud is the forte? The composer might indicate "allegro, forte," but the performer decides how fast and how loud because there is no single universal level of tempo or dynamics. The same is true of other diacritical markings such as crescendo, diminuendo (how fast will I get louder or softer?), agitato, and so on, even those that indicate articulations such as staccato (♩̣), or sostenuto (♩̱). For a staccato written ♩̣, the performer must decide if it is to be a short quarter or a long eighth, whether to stop the sound immediately before it or to glide into

---

[3]This term was devised by Guy Duckworth.

it. Other considerations include the note's position within a measure, its position in a scale, and what affect is being depicted. Does this sound complicated? It is, but the endless possibilities are what make art music exciting and worthy of lifelong study.

However, very few young singers, or other musicians for that matter, are aware of the performer controls and seldom make conscious decisions about how to use them in their practice or performance. They wait for the teacher to make the decisions for them. Thus new students return week after week to the lesson having practiced in the same tempo (usually moderato even if the score indicates otherwise), using the same dynamic levels (usually mezzo forte), and the same articulations (what articulations?), and then complain that their practice is boring.

The exercises that follow can teach more than breath management or good tone production: they can also develop the ability to make conscious decisions about the performer controls. They most certainly should not be construed as being either a complete listing of the possible approaches, nor as being the only way to use Dalcroze concepts. They are here only to whet your interest and spark your imagination.

VOICE CLASSIFICATION

One of the first technical questions I ask myself about a new student is, What is the student's voice type? Voice classificiation is an extremely important subject because great damage can be done by misclassification.

Since I usually teach undergraduates, most of whom are teenagers, I categorize them as late adolescents. Their voices will likely change dramatically from their freshman through senior year, so my impressions about their voice type remain tentative for some time. But I have to assign literature at some point, so it is helpful to know if I should start with a high, medium, or low category.

The exercise I use is quite simple:

> **1. "Place your hand on your chest and say your name loudly."**

Most people will typically use their lowest register when speaking. With an individual student, I ask if he felt anything happening in his chest as he said his name. If his answer is no, I ask him to repeat the exercise until he feels something, *anything*. I am starting the process of heightening his kinesthetic awareness by asking these questions and I am concerned that his answer reflects his experience. Usually, after several repetitions, the student will say he felt vibrations or buzzing. Once he can feel vibrations, with his hand still on his chest, he is ready for the next step.

> 2. "Beginning in the lower part of your speaking voice, say [a], loudly sliding up to your highest notes."

This step is repeated with a slower slide upward until a change is sensed, any change, in the amount or intensity of the vibrations in the chest.

I pay close attention to the approximate pitch(s) where the student senses a change in vibrations. This tells me where the transition is being made from the lowest register to another register.

> 3. "Starting where you experienced the change in vibrations, slide upward again, loudly on [a]. Repeat this step until you sense a second change in the amount or intensity of the vibrations."

I pay close attention again to the approximate pitch(s) where the second change occurs. Experience tells me that tenors and sopranos tend to change in similar areas (the tenor being an octave lower than the soprano), and mezzo sopranos and baritones also tend to change in similar areas (again, an octave apart). Bass-baritones tend to change slightly lower, and contraltos and bassos lowest of all.

The exercise gives me some information about which voice type I might be dealing with (notice I wrote, "might," since conditions are highly variable), and alerts the singer that her physical sensations are important. Classification of voices (tenor, mezzo, etc.) will become very important as studies continue. Gean Greenwell, whom I quoted in Chapter 1, believed that misclassification of voices was frequent and destructive, so I choose to err on the conservative side when classifying them. "You have to find your own backyard and stay in it," he used to say.

You will find a registration chart which Greenwell developed in Appendix B. I have included it because it partially explains some of the technical problems I frequently encounter. I hope you will find it useful.

BREATHING

We turn to breathing, also known as "breath control" or "breath management." I assume you already use or teach the type of breathing used by professional singers, commonly called "diaphragmatic breathing." The question is, What are the goals of breathing techniques? The list of answers would include, control and coordination of muscles in order to successfully complete the musical phrasing. A Dalcrozian would add, at all tempos, all dynamics, and using various articulations.

The five-note scale will serve to illustrate some of the exercises, but you may use almost any composition or other exercise.

Many teachers use the five-note scale with various syllables and consonants. It is common to extend the breath by exact repetitions. I use this form of the exercise, but with changing dynamics (mezzo piano to forte, forte to mezzo piano, etc.), and changing tempos (moderato, allegro, adagio, etc.).

Changing articulations within one breath is instructive as well. Be sure to vary the tempo with each repetition.

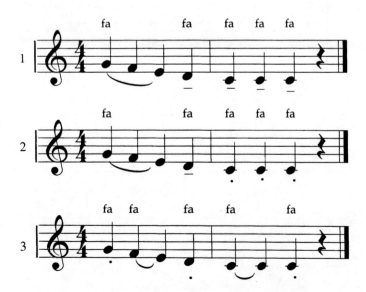

more difficult variations are

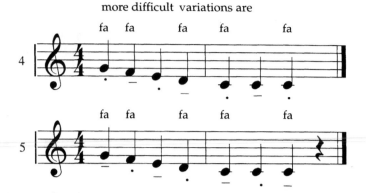

Notice the second measure of the third example above. This forces the singer to count during the longer note, something which few novice singers do.

Add changing dynamics to the varying articulations and varying tempos, and the exercise quickly becomes more complicated.

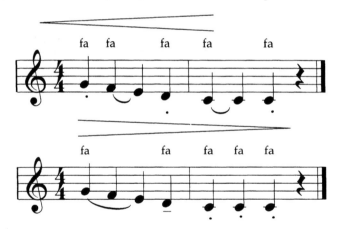

Sing the following:

Clap and breathe on every third beat: breathe *only* on the third beat (this means the pitch will not be sounded).

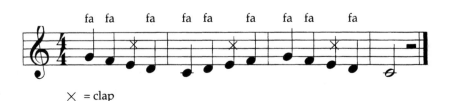

✗ = clap

> Put in the third beat; breathe and clap on the second. Breathe and
> clap on the first beat. Breathe and clap on the first beat of the first
> measure, the second beat of the second measure, the third beat of
> the third measure.

What did you discover? Was it difficult to remember when to
breathe and clap? Did you have difficulty finding the correct pitch of the
note following the clap? An outcome of this exercise is that you will learn
not only to control when you breathe, but that you have to internalize the
pitch you omitted in order to reenter accurately.

These exercises can be placed into your literature and can become
as elaborate as your imagination will allow. Here is a familiar song, Frère
Jacques (Brother John) in its bare essentials. Nothing is indicated about
tempo, dynamics, or articulation. I have omitted the text so you can sing
either the French or English version. Feel free to transpose it as well.

Now, turn this into an exercise for learning to control breathing.
Clap and breathe *only* where the x's occur.

Did you have difficulties finding the melody after the clap? This exercise also strengthens your inner hearing. You can make the exercise more complicated by adding dynamics and varying the articulation. These exercises may be performed with any literature.

ARTICULATION

I have already introduced the concept of articulation. Remember, by articulation, I am not referring to diction (that is another subject but closely related). *Articulation* refers to the sense of movement between the pitches and what happens as the pitch is attacked, how it is sustained, and finally how it is released as the voice moves to another pitch. Articulation is closely related to plasticity.

Words that describe articulation include float, glide, press, punch, skip, hop, jumping, lift, dab, slide, step. The musical terms for these movements include legato, sostenuto, staccato, marcato. The movement of articulation is closely related to levels of energy, such as energetic, lazy, placid, calm, tranquil, forceful, soft. The musical terms for these states of energy include tranquillo, forte, piano, mezzo piano, leggiero, pesante.

Here is Frère Jacques again with articulation added.

Here is the piece again with performer controls of dynamics and articulation indicated. I am not suggesting it *should* be sung this way, but rather that you can experiment with the performer controls. Notice the physical adjustments you must make in order to perform the piece. You may stumble along the way; if so, pay attention to what you have to do physically and mentally to recover.

Moderato

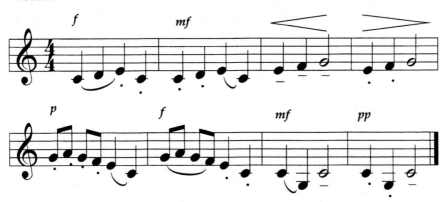

Transpose the piece both higher and lower to experience the new adjustments you have to make technically. Be sure to vary the tempos.

COORDINATING EAR AND VOICE

Warm-ups can serve to coordinate ear and voice as well as to activate vocal muscles. The following exercises are transposed up or down in your normal manner as the following directions are added:

You can continue using your favorite syllable (i.e., fa, li, re) and count on your fingers, or say the numbers.

1. Sing the scale normally.
2. Lower the third degree.
3. Back to normal.
4. Raise the fourth degree.
5. Back to normal.
   etc.

The order of the changes is not important. What is important is that you develop the feeling, the kinesthesia, of the changing scales, and pay attention to the places where the distances between the notes seem to demand a physical response. Use your hands to draw the scales in the air as your sing. Pay attention to how your voice responds to the changes.

5 4 3 2   1

The following exercises are variations on the same theme.

Change the rhythm and meter of the exercises.

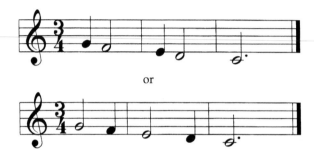

or

One of the goals of this simple exercise is to teach that each scale has its own way of moving, that changing the rhythms of the scales further alters that way of moving, that our voices can respond to those differences if we "hear" them with our bodies, not just our ears. It is my contention that many of the technical problems we encounter are a result of our bodies not understanding how to move through the varying scales (see Chapter 8).

COORDINATING EAR AND BODY

Occasionally a student will enter my studio and begin the lesson by telling me about a technical problem she is having in a section of one of her pieces. Rather than have her describe the problem, I ask her to sing that section so I can hear it.

Typically, she will sing until she arrives at the point where the problem occurs and then suddenly stop, saying that it always happens here. I point out that she stopped before the problem occurred, so I still do not know what the problem sounds like. It might take several more abrupt stops before she is willing to sing through the problem spot. It is important that she sing rather than tell me about the problem because spoken words cannot convey all the physical, acoustical, and musical information that singing can.

Fifty percent of the time, when she finally sings through the problem spot, she will experience no difficulty whatsoever, rather like having the toothache until you walk into the dentist's office. One possible explanation for this sudden change is that she began thinking about what she was doing, changing her physical response.

How did thinking about it help? When we encounter problems when singing, we often respond affectively ("It feels terrible," or "I don't like this feeling") and the analytical part of our brain shuts down as does our kinesthetic awareness. When we dissect the physical experience—we must have the experience first—we remove, or lessen, the affective reaction because by paying attention to the smaller, discrete components of the problem we break it into smaller, more manageable units. It stops being a giant looming over us and becomes, at second glance, a group of dwarfs on each other's shoulders. Have you ever had the experience of solving an apparently knotty problem simply by telling someone else about it? This was partly brought about by breaking it into smaller parts and removing the affect. When the student's technical problem suddenly disappears, I will ask her to recreate the problem anyway because she needs to understand how she resolved the problem or it will probably reoccur .

What about the other 50 percent of the time when the technical problem does not magically disappear? These are the times I look forward to because both the student and I will learn something.

Once the student has reproduced the problem, I analyze it aloud so she can hear what I am thinking. This is a way the teacher models the problem solving process which the student will eventually have to employ when the teacher is not present. The analysis will probably include both technical and musical possibilities. There might, in fact, be a readily detectable technical problem: her mouth might be nearly closed; she might be in the wrong register, mispronouncing a word, or the vowel might need to be modified.

Such obvious problems are fairly easy to remedy if the student can be made aware of them. Here's the rub: the teacher is aware of what the student is doing, but the student is not. The student is only aware of the unpleasant outcome, not what caused it. I discuss some methods for creating awareness in Chapter 13, so I will not linger on the subject here.

Very often faulty physical technique is only a part of a larger musical problem which typically falls under one or more of the following areas:

◆ The student does not understand the position of the beats within the measure, or harmonies or scales in the passage (ref. Chapter 8). Without this information, the student will not understand the shading and leaning necessary to efficiently produce the sounds (see Chapter 8).

♦ The student has trouble physically coordinating the rhythmic elements in the passage. The internal rhythmic "motor" may not be turned on. Without this internal sense of beat and rhythm, the student lurches from sound to sound, never knowing exactly when to start or stop. Physical tension is one outcome of rhythmic insecurity.

The second area is easy to test. The typical procedure begins with the following:

♦ The student claps the beat of the passage as she chants the melodic rhythm.

♦ The student then speaks the beat as she claps the melodic rhythm.

♦ The student alternates between the steps when I say, "Switch."

Occasionally, I will ask the student to perform the same steps, but add her feet to her voice and hands and move around the studio, alternating the beat and melodic rhythm between the three.

Rhythmic problems almost always make themselves evident during this process. We continue these and related procedures until she has coordinated and internalized the rhythm of the passage.

I will ask the student to sing the passage again and 90 percent of the time her vocal muscles will have worked through the problem. The student's body has taught her voice! Occasionally, at this moment, a student will look at me with a sense of wonder that is most gratifying. It also allows me to pontificate that the body is very smart, perhaps smarter than the brain, and it is certainly quicker. Rather than me imparting some magical solution for her problem, she has learned the "dance" of the passage.

I will ask her to do one final thing before we move on: perform the passage in the new way, then the old way. We will alternate the two performances until she has a strong kinesthetic sense of the new use of her muscles. The last step is based on this principle: if you don't know what you've changed, how can you be sure of what you've changed or that you will ever repeat it again?

AFFECT AND ITS EFFECT ON TECHNIQUE

I encourage you to introduce affect as early as possible in the learning process. There is an interesting question regarding affect and physical response: does physical gesture cause or motivate affect, or does affect inform the physical gesture (in this case the term includes the response of the vocal mechanism)?

Perhaps which causes which is less important than the fact that both need to be addressed. The effect on technique will be dramatic, even on warm-ups. You can make up flash cards, each with one emotion or attitude on it. I have included a short list in Appendix A, "Suggestions for Learning a Score Musically."

Introducing affect leads to a changed thought process. Rather than thinking, "Oh no, here comes the high note," the thought becomes, "What am I expressing?" The high note is not forgotten, but the body responds and coordinates itself in response to the affect. I have had occasion to attend sports events with both male and female students who assured me that "I can't sing that high" when working on a piece of music, only to hear them enter the vocal stratosphere in the excitement of the game. Their excitement prompted their vocal muscles into action.

Several years ago, public television televised interviews with pianists competing in the Tchaikovsky Competition. A Russian pianist, as usual, won the competition, and the other pianists were asked why they thought the Russians always did so well. Their answers varied, but almost all of them mentioned that the Russians seemed to see pictures as they played, as if they participated in a story they were telling with their music, whereas the other competitors spoke of thinking about their technique or visualizing the score.

My experience has been that the coordinating process between affect and body is quick and almost without effort; the effort comes when the brain tries to overcome the body and redirect its actions without changing the original affect. Redirection of the body by the brain will be facilitated by either changing the affect (e.g., angry into elated) or shading the affect (e.g., angry into bitter).

For example, a male student described the affect of a troublesome passage as "happy." Try as we could, we were unable to resolve a technique problem in that passage. We had almost given up when his pianist, who had been looking through my set of attitude cards, suggested we try "jolly." We spent a minute exploring the differences between "jolly" gestures and sounds and "happy" gestures and sounds. The singer repeated the passage in a "jolly" way and the technique problem disappeared. [4]

I learned a great deal in that moment: the earlier the redirection of the physical technique is connected to an affect, the easier the process. Words from the teacher tend to prolong the process of redirection, so the greater the number of words, the longer the process. This is why Dalcroze insisted that music teach music; musical behavior, on the teacher's

---

[4]The change probably occurred because the singer's physical response to the different affect was just different enough to change his muscular use.

part, facilitates the learning of new musical and technical behavior on the student's part because few words from the teacher are needed.

Prepare a number of affect flash cards.

Choose an affect at random as you sing either a warm-up or a section of a composition.

It is not important if the affect is appropriate to the music. In fact, experimenting with affects that are quite different from what you believe fits the music will lead to new insights about the importance of changing and shading affect within the course of the song. For example, smiling as you sing a sad song can give the effect of "smiling through your tears," a proven theatrical device for tugging at your audience's heartstrings.

Choose at least two affects. Alternate the affects as you sing a section of a composition.

Pay attention to any changes in your gestures and technique as you alternate the two randomly.

Choose at least three affects. Memorize them. Alternate them as you sing a longer composition from memory.

This exercise works better if someone other than you gives the command to change. You might find it difficult at first to remember both the composition and which affect you are switching to. Remember, it is better to have the experience and have difficulties than not to have the experience. You will learn more about memorization and technique from your difficulties than you will from your successes.

Use your affect cards in conjunction with the improvisation exercises in Chapter 7 and the earlier exercises in this chapter.

THREE METHODS OF PROCESSING INFORMATION

Humans, it seems, have many traits in common. Among these traits are the three basic ways we take in and process information from the world around us:

1. Aurally. We use our ears to take in information. When asked to recall the information, the person who unconsciously prefers the aural mode will access the aural cortex of the brain to recreate the sounds associated with the memory, rather like playing a tape recording.

2. Visually. We use our eyes to take in information. When asked to recall the information, the person who unconsciously prefers the visual mode will access the visual cortex of the brain to recreate the images associated with the memory, rather like seeing pictures. This is also known a "eidetic" memory.

3. Kinesthetically. We use physical sensations to take in information: touching, tasting, movements that are felt internally if not externally.[5] When asked to recall the information, the person who unconsciously prefers the kinesthetic mode will access the portions of the brain that control movement and recreate the muscular contractions and releases associated with the memory.

Of the three modes, I personally gravitate to the visual. I say things like "I see what you are saying" when someone explains something to me. If I do not have a mental picture of the event or idea, then I do not understand it. One of my goals in learning a musical composition is to learn in each of the three modes. When I am in a performance, I want to have all three working in case something happens to one or more of them.

I used to think that I really knew a composition when I could visualize it, and I was satisfied with that. However, several years ago during a public performance of a composition in English, I turned the page inside my head only to discover it was blank, white as the new fallen snow. After a split second of panic, I began making up the words and melody. The pianist accompanying me stuttered once at the keyboard as she tried to find out where I was in the printed score. She quickly realized I was creating my *own* score, so she began improvising in the style of the composer while valiantly trying to stay with my improvisation. After several measures, she and I had modulated to where we

---

[5]Musicians and athletes often refer to skills developed through repetition and remembered by the body as "muscle memory."

should be in the score, so she played a chord she hoped I would recognize. Fortunately, I did and found my place again. Later, I timed the improvised measures as I listened to a recording of the performance; it had lasted only twelve seconds, but they were some of the longest twelve seconds of my career.

I have also had the experience of performing music I learned when I was younger, and I am constantly struck by how long, and how well, my vocal muscles remember the composition, usually to my dismay. My muscles remember with great accuracy how they performed the piece years ago, even if the performance was far from wonderful. Even though my musical and vocal abilities have changed, for the better I hope, in the intervening years, my muscles are very reluctant to give up the old ways. This is why, when preparing an "old" composition, I often have to spend more time than with new literature.

As you study the modes, it will become important to determine which mode you prefer. The psychological approach known as Neuro Linguistic Programming™ (NLP), developed by Richard Bandler and John Grinder, can provide many insights and is well worth studying. I recommend *Frogs into Princes* as an introduction to their work.

Discovering Your Favorite Mode

Give yourself the following directions and pay attention to your physical responses, particularly the manner in which you use your eyes:

> **Visualize a familiar object, face, or scene.**

Did your eyes move up and to the left or right? Perhaps your eyes did not move, but rather became unfocused.

> **Visualize yourself wearing polka dot tights and a blue wig.**

Did you eyes move up and to the left or right (the direction will probably be the opposite of the remembered image in the first exercise)? Did they become unfocused? These first two questions are designed to allow you to understand how you access your visual mode.

> **Inside your head, listen to your favorite singer.**

Did your eyes move either left or right? Listen to your voice in your head. Where did your eyes move? Obviously, we are accessing the aural mode.

> **Imagine yourself in a warm bath or shower. Feel the water flowing over your body.**

Did your eyes move down and to the left or right? Now imagine a wonderful smell or taste. This is the kinesthetic mode.

As you worked through the exercises, did you find yourself stuck in one mode? For example, if you are visually oriented, you might have tried to see yourself in the shower or seen your favorite singer. There is nothing wrong with relying on one mode, but experiment with the other modes as you access all three modes for your learning. This will take a bit of doing on your part, since working in our least-used modes feels strange.

In my experience, singers who have trouble learning and memorizing are usually stuck in one mode or access the wrong mode. For example, they try to access the visual mode as they listen, or access the kinesthetic mode as they attempt to visualize the page.

Other examples of accessing the wrong mode occur in nonmusical settings as well. Good spellers, for instance, tend to access their visual memory when asked to spell a word; poor spellers, on the other hand, will access their aural or kinesthetic memories. One of the challenges of NLP is that people who use unsuccessful strategies—like the poor spellers—can be taught the strategies of good spellers who access their visual memories. The same can be done for musicians who have learning problems.

Using all three modes while learning music allows us to feel secure and be flexible, since we "know" the music in several different ways. The following are basic exercises to access the three modes. Select a composition that you have been working on only a short time.

Aural

Sing only the first beat of each measure aloud, singing the remainder of the measure internally. Proceed through the composition in this manner. For an added challenge, sing only the second or third beat of each measure. Use the piano to keep you on track if necessary.

You will quickly discover what you hear internally and how well you hear it. Be sure not to berate yourself if you have trouble; the purpose of these and all the other exercises in the book are to give you new experiences to discover what you know and do not know. Enjoy the challenge. If you had a great deal of difficulty, play the first note of each measure on a piano.

Sing the first measure aloud, then sing the next measure internally, listening closely to your "inner voice." Proceed through the composition in this manner.

Sing every third measure (every fourth measure, every fifth measure, etc.) aloud and hear the other measures internally.

Sing only the first measure of each phrase (you will have to analyze the phrase structure).

As you progress through these exercises, you should find that your inner voice grows stronger. Pay attention to the quality of that voice and make it your ideal sound. Your ideal inner voice will eventually come to lead your outer voice.

" 'Before I sing a tone I must have thought it,' Luciano Pavarotti said recently. . . . [He] did not say: before I start singing I assume good posture and take a deep breath with my diaphragm; then I bring my larynx and the tongue in the correct position; I open the mouth adequately and lift the velum, and start the sound by a firm contraction of the abdominal wall" (Günter, p. 4).

Visual

Repeat the preceding exercises, beginning with just the first phrase. However, close the score as you work. As you listen to your inner voice, visualize the score as clearly as you can.

As you work through these exercises, be sure to move your eyes to the "visual access" position you discovered as you worked through the exercises in Discovering Your Favorite Mode.

Kinesthetic

You have possibly already discovered that when you internalized the aural and visual modes, your internal kinesthetic sense was activated. Any muscle contraction or relaxation, any sense of the torso or throat muscles responding to the music playing in your head—all of these sensations are grouped under the rubric of kinesthesia. *The development of internal kinesthesia is one of the primary goals of eurhythmics.* Learning the internal "dance" of the music allows all the elements of physical and expressive technique to merge and be communicated to the audience.

In learning a new piece, it is often necessary to externalize the "dance" to strengthen the internal dance. To do this requires the external use of the large muscles to train the smaller muscles.

Working one phrase at a time, move around the room using your torso, arms, and feet to draw the music you hear in your mind. Pay attention to dynamics, tempo, quality of beat (heavy, light, floating, gliding, etc.), harmonies, and melodic movement (stepwise, skips, etc.).

This exercise can be performed without using your singing voice. Find ways to practice and learn music while saving your singing voice. Most of the singers I have worked with over the years maintain that the only way they can learn and memorize their music is to sing it over and over until it is beaten into their heads. This kind of rote learning is tedious and inefficient. Our brains are wired to work quickly and will "wander" after two or three repetitions of a pattern.

Using the Three Modes Together

"I have trouble memorizing words" is a common complaint among singers. I discuss ways to read scores musically in Chapter 12: the exercises you will find there are also very helpful in the memorization process. But before we leave this section, here is one more exercise that will pull together the three modes.

> **Without referring to the score, write the text as you quietly sing the melody out of rhythm.**

Little needs to be said about this exercise because once you try it you will discover how the three modes work together. You might also have found yourself constantly glancing at the score; fight that urge! In those moments of uncertainty or "blankness," your brain is furiously looking for the answer by searching its "memory banks," rather like the internal memory of a computer. Be patient and allow your brain time to find the missing piece of the puzzle. If necessary, skip the part you cannot remember and go on to the next thing you *can* remember. In most circumstances you will not facilitate the memorization process by constantly glancing at the score because you are not forcing your brain to work, and you will probably have to look it up again.

THREE FORMS OF KINESTHESIA

I have written a fair amount about kinesthesia in this chapter. The subject of kinesthesia is made even more complex because it comes in three flavors: unconscious, conscious, and imagined.

Unconscious and conscious kinesthesia are used every day of our lives. Any new task, for example, learning to walk, skip, read, write, or drive, begins with conscious kinesthesia. The task might be awkward at first, but once our bodies have mastered the activity we stop thinking about it and we move it to unconscious kinesthesia.

If you commute to work, the first day you commuted you probably had to consciously look for street names, building numbers, and perhaps make note of many details on your route. Before long, you probably began your commute by starting the car or boarding the train, and then began thinking about a myriad of other things. On the subway in New York City, I have watched commuters enter the car, take a seat, fall promptly asleep, then spring awake at precisely the right stop and leave the car. Their unconscious kinesthesia is on full alert. Conscious kinesthesia provides the way for our bodies and brains to learn the task; unconscious kinesthesia allows us to put repeated activities on automatic pilot so we do not have to make conscious decisions every time we perform an ordinary task such as putting on our clothes or brushing our teeth.

If, however, you break a leg or arm, you will find unconscious kinesthesia suddenly becoming conscious. Just getting into the car or boarding the train becomes a chore. But if you stay in the cast long enough, even that will become unconscious again.

All music study uses kinesthesia in at least two of its three forms. As singers, when we learn a new technique or composition, we begin with conscious kinesthesia. When we say we have learned a technique or composition, we mean we have moved most or all of it into unconscious kinesthesia so we can allow our attention (conscious kinesthesia) to focus on other activities. During a performance, if that conscious focus continues to be related to the information stored in the unconscious kinesthesia, then we usually feel we are performing well, since we are free to play with the material as it emerges. If we move too much into the unconscious, then we are on automatic pilot and the performance can become perfunctory and dull; on the other hand, if everything is conscious, we can feel out of control and unprepared.

The third form, imaginary kinesthesia, has probably been used by musicians for many years, but we have only recently given it a name. Some years ago, trainers of world-class athletes began using imaginary kinesthesia as a regular part of their training. Athletes are taught to imagine themselves performing their sport; they feel their bodies hurling down the slopes or pole vaulting as their muscles are trained by their minds. Singers can do the same. They can feel, see, and hear themselves in the ideal performance, or can be taught to predict and deal with distractions if they are prone to anxiety.

Dalcroze taught that there was a sound for every motion, and a motion for every sound; placing that concept into an imaginary kinesthesia allows singers to imagine their sounds coming to life. In their imagination, they can, for example, create dancers responding to their singing, or an infinite number of colors swirling.

I often direct singers to imagine their audience moving to the music. How would they want them to move? In my studio, singers will sometimes "conduct" with their voices, and I will move to show how I hear their music. Sometimes I will conduct the singers and they will interpret my movements with their sounds. We are turning sound into gesture and gesture into sound.

This is why I do not slight technique in my teaching, but rather am always searching for ways to direct it outward. "What do you want your audience to feel? How do you want your audience to move?" are questions my students hear often. Their response shades their sound, which in turn shapes the direction of their technique at that moment in the composition.

A Dalcrozian constantly looks for ways to enlarge the repertoire of the conscious kinesthesia because that automatically enlarges the range of choices by the unconscious. The imaginary kinesthesia then has a broader selection to choose from when it is called on. A reason for all of this emphasis on kinesthesia is that a goal of eurhythmics is to produce a clear and compelling performance in which the singer has learned the dance of the music and then is able to stand quietly and make the souls of the audience dance and sway.

I have given you brief overview of teaching technique, learning a score, and memorization using principles based on eurhythmics. It is not exhaustive and there are gaps I am tempted to fill, but I want to keep this book a reasonable length. I learned some years ago to stifle the urge to teach everything I know within one lesson. The same will have to be true for this chapter.

◆ Chapter 12 ◆

putting it all together: creative practicing

Robert Abramson, the premier eurhythmics teacher in America for a number of years, has, half seriously, proposed writing a book titled *Reading Music Will Kill Your Soul!* Perhaps the sequel could be *Practicing Can Kill Your Soul.* We form our feelings and concepts about music and develop our technique in the practice room, yet so much of our practice is undirected and boring. This is partly a result of thinking that repetition—also known as learning by rote—is the only way to learn.

Throughout my years of teaching, I have often had students bring different literature into their lessons and proclaim, "I hate this piece. It's boring!" When I ask how they are practicing, they respond, "I just go over and over it until I pound it into my head!"

Fortunately, I can tell them there is a better way to practice. Our brains are wired so that after approximately two exact repetitions our attention begins to wander. Notice I wrote "exact repetitions"; this is because any deliberate change in a pattern will produce attention. Our brains are wondrous, quick creations, yet we tend to treat them as if they were slow lethargic masses between our ears. Rote practice has the effect of slowing our learning; during a given practice period, the more we practice by rote, the less we learn. Changing our practice by setting tasks that demand our attention will turn drudgery into interest. Practice can become challenging and exhilarating.

Before we go further into this chapter, it will be helpful to you to know the principles that underlie the exercises that follow. [1]

[1] If you happen to be teaching adolescents or young adults, then you probably know you will often need to teach the students how and what to practice. I consider the first year a student works with me to be directed primarily to assessing, developing, and improving practice skills. Some come to me with excellent practice habits, but most do not. I have arrived at the assumption that how and what I want the student to practice must first be taught in the studio. Consider making the same assumption about your students.

IMPORTANT PRINCIPLES

We Learn Quicker When We Are Proactive

Refer to Chapter 7 for the definition of *proactive*. Proactive behavior puts us in charge of our practice and learning. Proactive behavior allows us to interact with the score rather than simply reacting; when the composer, for example, indicates forte, we can question why and experiment with different levels of forte.

Learning and Memorizing Are the Same Function

I do not separate these activities because looking at a score too long makes us "eye-bound." The eyes take in the information that then passes through the mouth without being heard or remembered.[2] Nothing is internalized.

I provided myself with an example of being eye-bound recently. I was preparing a group of new songs for a recital and, as I practiced them over a period of several weeks, I continued to read them, having convinced myself that I was practicing efficiently and creatively.

The day arrived when I decided I had to wean myself from the score, so I closed the score and began to perform them. To my bewilderment, I came to a screeching halt: I could not remember anything—the key, the language, the meter, nothing! I had learned—again—the results of being eye-bound.

I was reminded of why I inflict the torture on my students of performing their music without a score, at least once, during a lesson. Our ears and memories do not work so long as we are eye-bound.

Learn Music Using All Three Modes:
Auditory, Kinesthetic, and Visual

Refer to Chapter 11 for an analysis of the modes.

Set Goals to Help Organize Practice Time

Specific goals give us ways to measure our progress. Setting specific goals for each session will assist in using the practice time well. I say "specific" because goals which are too broad or general, such as "I want

---

[2]This term was created by James Froseth, head of music education, University of Michigan.

to sing better" or "I will start memorizing my music," will simply waste time. A more specific way of stating a goal of memorization would be, "I will be able to recite and sing the lyrics of the Caccini at the end of the next twenty minutes."

Incidentally, practice sessions of fifteen to twenty minutes are usually best for maintaining a high level of concentration. Singers who are under twenty years old should limit their singing to two or three short sessions daily or they risk damaging immature vocal muscles.

Find Ways to Practice Without Constant Singing

Practicing does not always mean singing. Tasks such as memorizing, working on pronunciation, analyzing phrasing and form, or working out rhythmic difficulties do not require constant singing. Practicing without constant singing will keep your voice fresh. Most of the exercises in this chapter may be practiced outside of the practice room. I occasionally tell my students, "Don't practice harder or longer; practice smarter." Singers can practice several hours a day and emerge vocally fresh.

Apply the Performer Controls Early

The performer controls (refer to Chapter 11) are dynamics, tempo, and articulation. Applying them early in the learning process encourages proactivity as we move through the early learning stages. Using the performer controls also stimulates the affective response and generates creative curiosity. It is quite easy to become mechanical as we struggle with the score unless we continuously search for ways to keep the creative juices flowing.

Form a Gestalt Early in the Learning Process

Gestalt is a German term meaning "form" or "shape." Rather like working a puzzle, finding the framework of a composition makes it easier to begin placing the myriad other pieces; by grasping the form (e.g., ABA or strophic) early, we can more easily fit the parts of the musical puzzle together. The gestalt process also encourages the use of metaphors[3] as a means of developing the affective colors of a piece. This process is sometimes referred to as "holistic."

---

[3]"The concepts that govern our thought are not just matters of the intellect. They also govern our everyday functioning down to the most mundane details . . . the way we think, what we experience, and what we do every day is very much a matter of metaphor" (Lakeoff, p. 3).

You may be familiar with some or all of the following exercises, since they have been developed by many teachers over the years. However, the sequence of the exercises is almost as important as the exercises and appears in three general steps:

◆ First, the exercises begin without specific pitch. Adding pitch to rhythm and text is difficult: either the pitch suffers (this is often experienced as physical discomfort and strain), the diction suffers, or, most frequently, the rhythmic vitality is reduced to timing.

◆ Second, pitch is added to text and rhythm, but only *spoken* pitch, not sung pitch. All the rules of accent, phrasing, and nuance (see Appendix A) can be applied before adding the written pitches.

◆ Third, the singing voice is added.

Once you are familiar with the exercises, you will discover you may rearrange them and add or skip them as the process becomes clear. If you are a teacher, I strongly urge you to work through these exercises before asking your students to try them. The problems you encounter, and the feelings you have, will probably be similar to those of your students. Remember, the goal is not to completely succeed the first time—you will learn very little if the exercise was too simple for you—but to enjoy the struggle because that leads to new levels of accomplishment.

Create a character and setting.

If the composition is in a language you do not speak, be sure to translate it, then ask questions like these:

> Are you the character in the piece?
>
> Are you describing, narrating, the action?
>
> Are you telling a story in the first person or third person?
>
> Where is the character: indoors, out of doors, in a city, in a forest?
>
> How old are you? Is the setting in the present or the past?
>
> What is your social class?
>
> What are you wearing?
>
> Are you being introspective, thinking aloud?
>
> Are you addressing another person, a group of people?
>
> Are you talking to friends, enemies, strangers, your sweetheart?
>
> What were you (as the character) doing immediately before you began telling this story? Eating dinner? Running through the forest?

All of the questions are designed to evoke feelings and spark the imagination. The questions relating to class and dress lead to exploring how the character moves; this has a direct effect on tempo and nuance.

```
Create a subtext.
```

After you have formed a gestalt and asked questions like the ones just listed, you are ready to think like the character who is singing. We use subtexts in almost all of our daily interactions with other people, and in most situations we do so on a subconscious level. For example, if you buy a hot dog from a vender, this might be your subtext:

> "I could really go for something to eat right now. That smells good! I wonder how much it costs? I don't see any prices listed. Does this guy speak English? His hands look dirty; I hope he uses those tongs . . . Three dollars! And I've already taken a bite! I can't give it back! Three dollars! This is outrageous!"

Meanwhile, the words you speak aloud might be these:

> "Gimme one, please. How much? That's more than I usually pay . . . You have a nice day, too."

Situations like the one described occur all the time, but as performers, we have to make them interesting, and subtexts can aid us immensely because we have to create them and then make them obvious to the audience through facial, physical, and vocal gestures.

THE EXERCISES

Choose a song that is new to you for the following exercises. Even though I suggest you work through the exercises on one composition, I strongly advocate working on several compositions at one time. Many people engage in "serial learning" in the early stages of study, that is, working on one work until it is "perfected" before beginning another. The result of this type of learning is that the person forgets the previous piece while working on the current piece and is always "between pieces," a state of affairs best avoided.

```
Begin with the text.
```

Assume the composer of a song had a text in mind before writing the music. This is not always true of pop composers, but is almost always true for composers of art song. The music to which the text is set is the aural result of the composer's response to the text. So the text seems the natural place to begin the examination of any song.

Read the text (or a translation of the text if one is available). What mood or emotion do you experience? Describe the moods or emotions you feel.

Describing the moods or emotions you feel is an increasingly difficult assignment because many people (1) do not know how they feel, and (2) do not have the emotional vocabulary to describe their feelings.

You have the opportunity to discover the infinite colors and flavors of the emotional spectrum. The typical response to the question, "How would you describe the emotions of this piece?" will be, "It's happy" or "It's sad," a rather limited emotional spectrum to say the least. Sometimes people will use words like "jerky, smooth, gliding, bumpy, heavy, light, soft, hard," which describe physical reactions but not emotional reactions. I recently had a student describe a piece as "happy." When I suggested to her that "happy" was fairly broad and asked if she could be more specific, she thought for a moment and said, "Real happy."

I believe our response to music reflects our responses and reactions to events and forces that shape our lives; we are with our music as we are with our lives. Linguists tell us that our vocabulary defines and limits our perceptions;[4] likewise, psychologists tell us that a lack of emotional vocabulary limits our ability to describe or perhaps even be aware of our various emotional states. This lack of emotional range reminds me of the critic who wrote that Katherine Hepburn's facial expressions "spanned the range of emotion from A to B."

You might have to expand your emotional vocabulary. If you do, you will be enriching your life in untold ways.

Form a gestalt.

---

[4]For example, Eskimos have more than seventy words to describe ice and snow but approximately four words describing events in time. People from Western European cultures have many words for time and have incorporated time concepts into the structure of our grammar, but we have few words to describe that cold wet stuff.

Listen to the entire piece. It is important to establish a gestalt of a new piece, since this not only gives you a feel for the piece, but also accelerates learning. I am usually able to hammer and slash my way through a new score at the piano; perhaps it is not pretty but it is useful. If you do not have any piano skills, recordings are helpful. Several recordings of the same work are preferable because the goal is to form a concept of the piece, not imitate someone else's performance. If there are no recordings available, then you might attempt to find a friendly pianist to play the piece for you.

Whatever the means you choose, pay attention to the feeling of the entire composition; follow the song by ear as much as possible rather than looking at the score.

Examine the composer's tempo markings (andante, largo, allegro, rallentandos, accelerando), dynamic markings, fermatas, sudden high or low notes. What do they tell you about the composer's feelings about the text?

What we call a "musical score" is the physical evidence of a composer's reactions to sounds which sprung from the inner hearing of the composer. The markings on the score result from the composer's efforts to use a commonly accepted code to convey thoughts and feelings. Simply re-presenting, or re-creating, the code is not enough to create an expressive performance because it does not bring insight into the emotional reactions of the composer.

TEXT
↑

COMPOSER
thoughts
feelings
compositional skill

↓

SCORE
↑

PERFORMER
thoughts
feelings
technique
(vocal)
(expressive)

The graph shown above gives a simplified depiciton of the ideal relationship between the composer and the performer. Performers, as re-creators, allow us to hear their interpretation not only of the code, but of the composers' and performers' personal reactions.

Imagine living in the days when the telegraph was the quickest form of communication, and you received a telegram from your sweet-heart which read:

· · ·   —   —   · ·   —   · · · ·   — — —   — —   — ·   — ·   — — —

Unless you read Morse Code, it looks like a series of dashes and dots and is devoid of meaning. You would probably stride into the tele-graph office and demand someone read it for you. If the clerk said, "Well, it says: dot dot dot dash dash dot dot . . ." you would be justified in feel-ing frustrated because he did not interpret the message but simply re-produced what was on the page. You want to know what words the dashes and dots represent.

If the clerk translates in a flat, computer-like voice, "We've just won the lotto," you might be surprised and pleased with the information, but your level of excitement would not be what it might have been. If the clerk's voice was lively and joyful ("We've won the lotto!!"), your level of excitement would be multiplied because of the clerk's personal reaction. The content was the same, but the performances—the way the content was relayed—were different.

The next exercise is designed to move beyond the dashes and dots and into the words the composer might have intended us to hear.

> **Speak the text in a dramatic fashion, as in a public performance. How many times did you breathe? What pitch range did you use in your speaking? Find your speaking pitches on the piano. Repeat the exercise and increase the range of the spoken pitches. Translate the text into your own words. Recite the text again using an emotion or attitude picked at random. How did the randomly picked attitude highlight or contrast the feelings in the text?**

Speak the text as poetry (or prose) in a dramatic fashion as you would in a public performance. This exercise is difficult since many young singers dislike poetry. This dislike usually springs from unfortu-nate experiences in schools in which teachers have had the students learn the *correct* interpretation of poems, meaning the teacher's interpretation. If you are a teacher, you might have to help students interpret the text without imposing your interpretation on theirs. Sometimes students offer complicated, offbeat interpretations. These interpretations usually come from high school teachers who insisted on a metaphysical meaning for the most mundane text. A student interpretation of "The sun was high, and I spied a flower on the edge of the road," might be, " I'm, like, middle-aged, old, you know, and I, uh, see this beautiful girl sitting, like, in an outdoor restaurant, maybe, having a drink?" I usually advise such a student to look for the most obvious answers.

How many times did you breathe? Sometimes singers will read a text, breathing in obvious places (commas, ends of sentences, etc.) without being aware they breathed at all. They will then proceed to sing through two or more phrases without breathing, only to gasp for breath in the middle of a phrase. They are unaware the composer builds places into the music that call for the sound to stop (phrasing). These built-in places usually coincide with word phrasing. Becoming aware of breathing points in the text alerts the student to similar breathing points in the music.

What pitch range did you use in your speaking? Singers frequently misuse their speaking voices by placing the speaking pitch too low (sopranos sometimes place them too high). Finding their approximate speaking pitch on the piano makes them aware that their voices have pitch (many people are, somehow, unaware of that fact). Morton Cooper, in his book *Change Your Voice; Change Your Life,* gives many fine exercises for discovering the best speaking pitch for a voice.

Repeat the exercise and increase the range of the spoken pitches. Repeating any exercise is a waste of time, in most cases, unless some thought and analysis has occurred between the repetitions. Setting a goal ("increase the range") is one way to make a repetition useful.

Increasing the range of the pitches used in the speaking voice will also incorporate an element of improvisation. Deliberately distorting the usual speech pattern will assist in finding new ways of using the voice, for example, changing pitch within a word, e l o n g a t i n g a word, playing with consonant sounds, or making usually long sounds short. Of course, if you are a teacher, you should be able to demonstrate.

Translate the text into your own words. If the text is in a language other than English, work out a literal translation. It is important that this be done very early in this process, since singing with understanding is an integral part of an expressive performance.

Translate the text into your own words, even if the text is already in English. Remember, one of our goals is to move from reactive behavior (simply accepting whatever words appear on the page) into proactive behavior (interpreting). Rather than assuming you understand the text, translate it; if you have a literal translation of a non-English text, translate the translation. For example, "I spied a fair damsel," might be translated

"I saw a pretty girl." This is an uninspired translation to be sure, but at least you would know that I understood the word "damsel." Putting the text in your own words allows you to make an affective connection with the text.

Recite the text again using an emotion or attitude selected at random. How did the randomly selected attitude highlight or contrast the feelings in the text? Too often, we work in an affective vacuum until we near a performance. This exercise will suggest to the student that the "feeling" of the text and music is an integral part of the learning process. An attitude that is quite different from the affect of the text and music will highlight the attitudes which the composer intended. A list of attitudes and emotions is included in Appendix A.

> **Speak the text following the melodic line, out of rhythm, using the musical rules.**

This exercise develops the understanding that spoken words have inherent qualities of beat, rhythm, pitch, and accent. It is also the most difficult exercise because so many musicians think the music is in the pitches. In fact, the pitches contain only a part of the music; the majority of the music is contained in the rhythms, dynamics, and structure of the composition. Following the musical rules will necessitate the examination of the formal structure and rhythmic makeup of the composition.

We all want to sing through pieces, not realizing that the sounds of our voices confuse us; we think we are using dynamic shadings and clear diction, but are fooled by the physical effort we are making to produce the sound. It is difficult to hold the urge to make singing sounds in check, but the more you internalize the musical elements of the performance, the more you will save your singing voice. We want to sing, sing, sing, when we should be listening, feeling, and thinking.

> **Speak the text in the rhythm of the music, being careful to vary pitch and dynamics, following the musical rules and the normative measure. What types of articulation did you use? Pay attention to the phrasing of the text as it relates to the phrasing of the music.**

Speak the text in the rhythm of the music, being careful to vary pitch and dynamics, following the musical rules. Most singers tend to speak the text in a flat, lifeless monotone (errhythm strikes again!). Record your performance to ensure your voice has not gone "flat."

Use the normative measure. If you discover that applying the musical rules in the context of a normative measure becomes difficult, if not impossible, then you are using the musical rules correctly. The function of the normative measure is to "normalize" the measure; the function of expression is to deviate from the normal. Changes from the normal are, by definition, expressive. The question is always, "What is being expressed?"

What types of articulation were used? Articulation is different than "good diction." For a Dalcrozian, articulation refers to the way a note is attacked, the quality of the duration, and its eventual release. For singers, the qualities of attacks are determined by the first letter of the word (consonant or vowel) and what happened at the end of the preceding word. The movement between the words, "I love you"—the "I" sliding into the "l" followed by sustaining of the "ove" which elide with the "y"—is quite different than the movement in "I hate you"—with the "I" followed by the aspirated "h" which quickly moves to the "t," which bites into the "y." But if those words appeared in the context of

| I | love | you | | I | hate | you |

all other musical elements being the same, the inexpressive singer will perform both legato because of lack of awareness that the words demand very different articulations.

Pay attention to the phrasing of the text as it relates to the phrasing of the music. Exploring the phrase structure of the composition began with the first exercise in this section (*"How many times did you breathe?"*).

SINGING MUSICALLY IN THE EARLY LEARNING STAGES

Now we come to the difficult part: singing musically while in the early stages of learning a composition. Singers want to learn the pitches, but learning pitches without reference to key, form, or harmony is like seeing many different colors (a green streak there, a red one here, a blue one there) without understanding that you are looking at an impressionist painting. Sight-reading musically involves improvisation and awareness of harmony and tonality: improvisation, because of willingness to miss a "pitch" and "go for the gesture"; harmony and tonality, because of the awareness that musical gesture lives within the framework of those two elements.

One part of the problem in the early learning stages is that usually, when a new task is being learned, we develop amnesia, forgetting all previous learning. Part of your task is to bring the previous learning back to consciousness. This amnesia is one reason young singers lose good voice quality when they are confronted with a new task; another reason has to do with fear of making mistakes.

I have alluded to mistakes often in this text. Teachers and students often think of them as something to be avoided at all costs, since they might represent a character flaw. They feel stupid when they make mistakes. Putting mistake avoidance as a high performance priority is a guaranteed way to ensure you forget all previous learning and concentrate on "getting the notes right"; it is also a good way to create performance anxiety. However, if you assume you will make mistakes as the number of tasks increases, you will become process-oriented, rather than product-oriented as learning unfolds. The performer using a gestalt approach does not overlook mistakes, endure sloppiness, or otherwise lower standards of performance, but rather views mistakes as part of the learning process and finds ways to correct the mistakes through musical means. The traditional "error-detection/error correction" approach and the gestalt approach both correct mistakes: the difference lies in how mistakes are analyzed and how and when they are corrected.

Another problem I encounter with sight-reading is that most of the students I teach are, at least in the early years, poor readers. As I work with them to develop their reading skills, I insist they read as musically as they can. They can still use a wide range of dynamics and pitch in their speaking voices and many types of articulations (e.g., legato, staccato, detached), as well as developing coordinated bodies; lacking reading skills makes them slightly handicapped, not musically disabled.

Earlier in this chapter I suggested you use a recording of the piece with the intent of developing a broad concept of the composition. If you are a teacher, you will also discover that some of the steps listed are superfluous for some students because they immediately use their speaking voices musically (singers who translate musical expression into their speaking voices, however, are very rare). These expressive students usually need only to be led through the musical rules and they will develop a quick grasp of the composer's style. Other students will need to be led through each step slowly. Remember, your goal as a teacher is to assist those students who are not naturally expressive (probably about 95 percent of our students) to become so. In short, you are teaching the student techniques of expression.

Suggested Steps

The following steps are designed for a teacher to use with students, but if you are working alone, and assuming you have some keyboard skills, you can adapt them for your private use as I have often done.

If you have worked through the earlier exercises and have begun incorporating expressive elements in your voice as you speak the text, then you are ready for the following steps.

Once again, play or sing the composition, this time following the score.

If you are a teacher, ideally you or a pianist will perform the composition, with the vocal line highlighted, as the student speaks the voice part, using all the musical rules of expression she can remember as she hears it played. This exercise assumes the pianist will also perform the piece expressively.

The intent is to form a gestalt that incorporates the expressive elements as quickly as possible, with little attention directed toward "getting it right."

Play the accompaniment in chords out of rhythm as you sing the melody. Roll (i.e., arpeggiate) the chords so you can hear all the notes.

Pay attention to subtle changes in the quality of your sound as you perform this exercise. These changes will occur as you intuitively adjust your technique to "get the right feeling." I alluded to this phenomenon in Chapter 9 in the discussion of rhythmic solfege.

A goal of this exercise is to become aware of how the voice part fits the harmony, allowing your voice to adjust to the changing scales. I am continually fascinated by the looks on students' faces when their voices suddenly adjust to accommodate the harmonies that support them. I personally experience an almost audible click, a feeling of settling into a groove, when my voice and body understand the musical scale I am singing. My students have other descriptions for what happens to them, but the effect is the same: reduced muscular effort, more "ring" to the sound, and a sense of flow with the music.

In performing this exercise, pay close attention to any sense of muscular holding you hear; this happens when the singer fights against or ignores the harmony surrounding the melody, what I call the harmonic matrix. This is most often an example of a musical problem (not hearing/feeling the harmonic matrix) disguised as a technical problem.

> Conduct yourself as you sing using the traditional conducting patterns.

Conducting yourself as you sing will clarify the meter. Rhythmic and metric mistakes you might be making will quickly become evident. Pay attention to moments when your arms become uncoordinated while conducting; this usually means your body does not understand the rhythm or meter.

> Improvise the text as you sing the printed melody. Improvise the melody as you sing the printed text.

Refer to Chapter 7 for exercises you can adapt for this process. Learning to improvise in the style of the composer can give you added confidence that you can handle any occurrence while performing. Learning to improvise text in your native language, one of the most difficult skills, will also aid you in overcoming the urge to stop the music because you forgot a word.

Suggestions for the Later Stages of Learning

Eventually you will sing from memory while working with a pianist. The first run-throughs will be difficult but necessary. You will probably need to sing through a piece from two to four times before you feel reasonably comfortable. I refer to these early run-throughs as "critical mass," rather like the amount of nuclear material needed for an atomic reaction. This is an important stage of the learning process because you and the pianist will quickly discover what you both need to learn. You will be tempted to use the score to avoid making mistakes rather than stumbling through; don't do it! Keep stumbling: you will discover what you know and what you need to learn. Use the following five-step score accuracy check.

◆ 1 ◆

> Sing the entire composition four, five, or six times slower than your regular tempo while looking at the score, preferably as you play your part on the piano.

This is a method of checking for accuracy, so avoid dynamic and range extremes. Sing quietly, sing an octave lower and take as many breaths as you need, since you will not be able to use your usual phrasing. Pay close attention to the score and make no assumptions about your accuracy.

◆ 2 ◆

> **Sing the composition four, five, or six times slower than your regular tempo *without* looking at the score.**

This is a method of strengthening your memory and concentration. Continue to sing as easily as possible.

◆ 3 ◆

> **Sing the composition at your normal tempo while looking at the score.**

This is another check for accuracy, but using your normal tempo will accelerate your thought processes. Sing as easily as possible.

◆ 4 ◆

> **Sing at your normal tempo *without* looking at the score.**

Continue to sing as easily as possible.

◆ 5 ◆

> **Sing four, five, or six times faster than your normal tempo *without* looking at the score.**

Sing easily. This exercise will force your memory to function quicker than will be required in performance. In addition to forcing your physical and mental muscles to work efficiently and rapidly, you will discover you are more able to deal with distractions during performance.

The final exercise is the incorporation of all the elements mentioned in this chapter through movement and singing. Now you have the information; it is up to you to put it to work.

One caveat: if you encounter problems on any of the steps, return to an earlier step. Coordinating technique, listening, and the musical elements (the musical rules, rhythm, dynamics, tempo, pitch) is a very complicated juggling act. When we have problems, we usually let go of the rhythm and become errhythmic; if we still have problems, we tend to ignore all nuance, accents, and phrasing. At this point, our muscles are so confused that they become spastic and arrhythmic and we stop singing, complaining that our technique is not working.

Developing practice skills is of vital importance, since we spend more time practicing than performing. Approaching practice efficiently and musically will lead to more musical performance.

◆ Chapter 13 ◆

three
sample
lessons

I present three sample lessons in this chapter to demonstrate how I use Dalcroze principles in different circumstances. The sample lessons are based on composites of lessons I have taught over the years. Teaching, like learning, is a process. The sample lessons illustrate the teaching activity and my related analysis (descriptive) rather than a step-by-step teaching technique, such as "when this happens, do this" (prescriptive). The musical or pedagogical principles appear in ***bold italic*** type.

While teaching, I attempt, with varying degrees of success, to keep the following concepts in mind:

◆ ***Music teaches music.*** Music is not about words, since no words can completely capture what happens within a musical performance. Therefore most lessons should be about music, not words: the less the teacher talks during a lesson, and the more the teacher becomes the music during the lesson, the better. Teaching is a performing art.

I am not always successful in implementing this concept because I occasionally catch myself yammering on while the student's eyes glaze over. However, when I stop talking and make music with the student, more learning always takes place.

◆ ***Excellent teaching teaches the student while the student wrestles with the material.*** To describe this approach to teaching would require another book, but briefly stated, using this approach, the teacher pays attention to the entire student and the learning style, attitudes about the task, reactions to challenges, and the overall physical approach to the task. Another term for this approach is "student-centered teaching."

Traditional teaching is "teacher-centered," meaning the musical goals and, occasionally, the teacher's ego, are the teacher's primary concern. This teaching is also authoritarian, with the teacher (the authority) setting the student's goals and determining the student's needs. Student-centered teaching does not deny the teacher's needs, but suggests ways that both teacher and student can combine their needs to create common goals.

◆ *The student's job is to do the learning; the teacher's job is to create the environment for learning to take place.* It has been written that the student will do everything possible to get the teacher to do the learning: don't do it! The student who has the same lesson week after week, who asks you to "show me again," repeatedly, who does not like to try anything until you have demonstrated several times is having you "do the learning." Whenever I feel this is happening, after I have repeated something more than twice, I stop and say, "I already know how to do that. You try it now."

◆ *Dalcroze methodology teaches musical behavior rather than teaching pieces or even concepts.* To a Dalcrozian, training ears, brains, and bodies to feel and hear what the eyes see is more important than teaching a series of pieces. Voice teachers often just want to train voices and teach "pieces" while disregarding the emotions, minds, ears, and bodies that are attached! This is a serious problem in our profession and one that will be with us so long as we remain technically oriented.

◆ *Don't confuse the teacher's need for comfort with the student's learning needs.* "My students need a lot of structure. I don't think they will be comfortable with this approach." This is a comment I often hear from voice teachers. The question is, who *really* needs the structure, and who is, in fact, uncomfortable with this less teacher-structured approach? Sometimes it is the student, but most often it is the teacher. When a teacher becomes frustrated and angry that a student is not doing well, the cause for the anger is often not the student but rather the little voice in the teacher's head that keeps saying, "maybe if I were a better teacher, this student would be doing better." This is what I mean by the teacher's ego involvement.

◆ *Mistakes create possibilities for learning.* Examine your attitude about mistakes. What do they mean to you? Teachers and performers who choose a gestalt approach need to have a fearless attitude about mistakes. For them, mistakes are opportunities for learning rather than signs of eminent failure.

◆ *Teachers do more than merely give directions.* In the Dalcroze philosophy, instructors give directions, lead students through exercises and point out mistakes; teachers, on the other hand, create an environment where students experiment with different skills and attitudes, and leave lessons with not only better skills but enlivened imaginations and a joy of making music. A Dalcrozian gives tasks that are within the grasp of the students, but which cause them to stretch to accomplish the tasks. Mistakes are viewed as doors to learning rather than potholes in the road to understanding.

Gean Greenwell provided wonderful examples of excellent teaching in many of our lessons. He was very pleased whenever I was performing well, but his eyes would sparkle when I encountered a problem. This was not from wishing me ill, but rather that he had an opportunity to teach me something. I recall observing another student's lesson where the student apologized for having a problem (this was an interesting comment on the student's relationship with his previous teachers). Greenwell chuckled and said no apology was necessary, and that he understood the student might be a bit frustrated, but he (Greenwell) was just starting to have fun because he finally had something to do!

◆ *What the student discovers, the student remembers.* This is actually, I think, an ancient Chinese saying, but it is still applicable to our teaching. Have you ever "fixed" an incorrect rhythm or interval, only to hear the same mistake week after week? The problem is that *you* discovered the mistake, but the *student* has not yet had the experience of its "mistakeness." The best way to fix the mistake is to create a situation where the student has the "aha!" revelation.

◆ *The map is not the territory: music lies within sound, not on the printed page.* Just as a map only represents a territory, so the printed score only represents the music. The music lies within the sounds that emanate from the person. The task is to discover how the person can best create the sounds, develop the aesthetic, technical, imaginative, and musical capacity to express them, and shape them according to the design the composer has indicated.

Now to the lessons.

FIRST LESSON WITH A NEW STUDENT

I'm sitting in my studio at the university waiting for Tom to arrive. I hear a soft knock on the open door and Tom enters, exactly on time. He is a first-semester freshman and this is the first lesson we will have together.[1] I have been looking forward to working with a new student, but Tom,

---

[1]Jaques-Dalcroze thought of the teacher as learning from the student; ideally, all the participants in a lesson share the roles of teacher/student.

understandably, seems to have some trepidation about having a new voice teacher.

Other things I know about Tom: he listed his voice type on his audition form as " bass," which is probably the part he sang in his high school choir and not necessarily his actual voice type; he is eighteen years old and probably undergoing the throes of the typical freshman who is away from home and making his own decisions for the first time.

Background

I ask him to be seated and tell me about his musical background and to describe his professional goals. His background is typical for many voice students: he had piano lessons as a child but quit after a few months, he was in the marching band and chorus in high school and enjoyed being a part of a musical ensemble. He had some private voice lessons with his school choral director as preparation for solo-ensemble festivals, but no outside study.

When I ask him about his professional goals, he says he wants to be a high school choral teacher, since he liked his director a lot. He says nothing about loving, or even liking music other than as a social activity. When I ask him what kind of music he enjoys listening to, he replies that "pop" and "rock" are what he usually prefers, but he sometimes likes "semiclassical" as well. When I ask him what he means by semiclassical, he explains that he means works such as *Phantom of the Opera* and *Les Miserables*.

Listening to his responses, I think about the work that lies ahead of us. He will have no understanding of genres of music he will be required to perform in order to satisfy the requirements of an academic setting, so he and I must find ways to make the music relate to his life experiences.[2] He also does not have a vocal role model, since he does not listen to trained singers, so I will have to find ways to clarify the aural goals of his study.

First Steps Toward Building a Vocal Image

"How does your voice sound to you, and what would you like it to sound like?" I ask him. No one has ever asked Tom this question before, so he takes a long time before replying. "It's kind of, you know, just there," he says. "I can't sing very high and I can't sing very soft. What would I like it to sound like? I guess I want to be able to sing higher and not have it hurt." I notice he has not said anything about his sound, only how it feels. Part of this inability to talk about sound comes from (1)

[2]Musical studies that are not related to the student's life experiences and feelings have little affective meaning to the student.

never being asked to talk about it and (2) lack of vocabulary.[3] Building an expressive vocabulary will be another part of our work together.

I have also noted the manner in which Tom has used his body during our talk, the energy level of his gestures, the pitch range and quality of his voice, any obvious physical tension; all of these elements help me form an image of Tom that will eventually be called into play during his lessons. This interview has taken only five or six minutes. Now I ask him to perform a couple of pieces he is comfortable with so I can have a better sense of his voice.

He says that he has three pieces, and waits for me to choose one. Instead, I ask him to pick one. This is a subtle way of making him take responsibility for his work (become proactive) rather than simply following directions given by the teacher (being reactive).

Lesson 1: How to Establish a Tempo

He chooses *Caro Mio Ben* by Giuseppi Giordani. I take the music and go to the piano. "What is your tempo?" I ask. "I don't know . . ." he replies. "It's kind of like this; one, two, three, four," he says, using a quiet voice to indicate an allegro. I play as he indicated, and he immediately stops me, saying it is too fast and too soft.

"Oh? Well, give me a better tempo and dynamic level," I say, and he gives the same tempo but louder dynamic level. I point out the tempo is identical to his first tempo. He tries again but the pulse is barely slower.

I suggest he sing the first line. Finally, he arrives at a tempo that is comfortable for him; it does not necessarily match any of the affect of the music, but I imagine his choral director always chose the tempo for him rather than helping him determine it for himself.

He sings the piece as if it were a slow march, bumping from note to note. The melody and metric rhythms are correct and the performance is lifeless: it is a typical errhythmic performance. I make a mental note to work on that, but I want to quickly make the act of singing a little easier for him because that is one of the goals he stated.

Teaching Technique Nonverbally: Encouraging Analysis

I had noticed that he barely opened his mouth while singing, so I ask him to watch. I mimic his performance of the opening passage (without

---

[3]One of the teaching goals of the Dalcroze methodology is appreciation of nuance. Nuance in language is the ability to express feelings and perceptions in fairly specific terms. Most students' vocabularies are limited to "happy-sad," " good-bad," or "fast-slow," and they have to be taught affective words (such as glib, exuberant, melancholy, elated) and descriptive words (such as sparkling, dull, bright, colorful, vibrant).

telling him I am reproducing his performance), then I repeat the passage, this time allowing my mouth to open more. I ask him if he sees or hears any difference between my performances. He says he hears a little difference. When I ask him to describe the difference, he says the first one is more "nasal" than the second.[4]

I repeat the performance, asking him to look for any differences. He does not see any, so I repeat again, pointing to my mouth (**directing his attention**). Finally he notices the effect of the jaw opening on the tone.

Problem: debauched kinesthesia;[5] developing awareness. I ask Tom to sing first with his mouth closed, then open. He sings the passage twice, but the amount of opening remains the same. I direct him to stand in front of a mirror and watch as he repeats the performances. As soon as he begins singing, he looks away from the mirror. I stop him and repeat the directions. He says he thought he *was* watching, but tries again.

This time he watches as he sings the passage twice, keeping his mouth almost closed both times. I ask if he saw any difference in how far his mouth was open. He replies that it felt different. "But did you see any difference?" I ask. "I don't know," he replies. I conclude that he cannot see, hear, and feel at the same time: when he feels, he cannot see; when he hears, he cannot feel *or* see. Of course, I have kept all of these observations of his awareness to myself, but they will be of value in helping me determine his curriculum.

I direct him to stand in front of the mirror and make some sounds with his jaw closed, then open. After a few seconds, I ask him to simply speak the words of the passage he has been singing; it quickly becomes apparent that he does not remember the words without the melody. Internalizing music and text will be one of the first skills I will attempt to teach him in coming lessons.

Problem: ignorance of the meaning of the text; absence of affect. Before returning to the kinesthesia exercise, we look at the score and I ask if he knows what the words mean. "Not really," he says ("not really" in student jargon means "no"). "Do you like this piece?" I ask. He looks at me as if he has never considered that question. "Not really," he replies.

"Then why are you doing it?" I ask. Again, that look as if I had just arrived from Mars. "Because my teacher said it would be a good

[4]Nonverbal performance, which demands attention, followed by analysis, help develop two necessary skills for the successful musician.

[5]A majority of people are unaware of how they use their bodies. It is necessary to reestablish kinesthetic awareness.

audition piece." I give him an option: we can continue working on this piece or he can choose one of his other pieces. He chooses *Passing By* by Edward Purcell. "It's kind of a boring piece," he says, "but I like it better."

Tailoring the Teacher's Agenda to the Student's Needs

Rather than continue with the kinesthesia exercise in its present context, I decide to shift it into another form. Tom performs *Passing By* and, while the performance is still errhythmic, there is some improvement in his sound. He is quicker in noting the difference in sound, as well as feeling, when he opens his mouth more. He also has a better sense of the meaning of the text, since it is in a language he understands, and we begin speaking the words, "There is a lady sweet and kind," playing with their sounds and feelings, such as the vocative of "th" of "there," the "z" of "is" that slides into "a" creating a "za," which, in turn, tapers into the "l" of "lady" (I have him perform the American "l" and the European "l" to sense the difference in tongue position).

I call his attention to the sensations in his tongue, lips, and jaw as he plays with the words, and ask him about his feelings about the words. He still has no particular emotional connection with the text, so I ask him to visualize the most beautiful girl he could imagine and we explore—with some embarrassment on his part—how he might react to seeing such a woman pass by and, in an instant, change his life. I have him sing the first verse again, this time while attempting to use all the emotions and sensations he has discovered. Of course he cannot keep all the changes, but there are small improvements in his sound.

Testing

I ask Tom to repeat his first performance again. "I can't remember how I sang it," he says. To help him remember, I guide him back to his first performance by reproducing what I remember. Then he repeats the "new" performance and I ask him to change between the old and new performances when I say "change."[6] We continue the exercise until he starts laughing at the troubles he encounters juggling the two performances.

---

[6]How do we know what we have changed unless we can remember what we did? If the student cannot reproduce both the original performance and the changed performance, the teacher may assume the changes will have to be taught again.

Summary

I ask Tom what he has learned during our few minutes together and he mentions the need to open his mouth more and to find out what the words mean before he brings a piece into a lesson. We talk about literature requirements and collections he should purchase. After he leaves, I review the lesson and realize we will have to look at his inefficient practice habits very soon.

This lesson has been about developing awareness. Tom is not unusual in his lack of awareness of self-perception, so every lesson for the foreseeable future will have to incorporate activities that focus on awareness. Much of his progress in developing musical and technical skills will hinge on this ability to become aware.

The lesson also touched on several important musical and technical elements in a very cursory manner, but basic musical behaviors such as paying attention, concentrating, and remembering and reproducing the sounds were the major focus.

LESSON WITH A SECOND-YEAR STUDENT

Background

Cindy, a sophomore performance major, has been studying with me since coming to the university and has presented many challenges for me as a teacher. Two years ago, she sang a very nice audition in which she displayed a lovely young soprano voice. The voice faculty was enchanted with her and counted her as one of the bright new members of the freshmen class. However, during her first lesson with me, I discovered she did not read music. She told me her previous voice teacher had spent a year teaching audition repertoire to her by rote. So I had unwittingly taken on the task of teaching a bright, ambitious young singer with a lovely voice who was musically illiterate. I needed to find ways to teach her to read and to help her develop her musical and technical skills, all the while keeping her quick intelligence and natural exuberance engaged in the process.

Her musical tastes far exceeded her abilities. During her first year, she would bring in arias from operas she had discovered and fallen in love with ("Sempre libera" from *La Traviata* by Verdi, and "Der Hölle Rache" sung by the Queen of the Night in *The Magic Flute* are two I vividly remember) while struggling to understand how to perform simple dotted rhythms in her lessons!

Her lessons during her first semester consisted of the following:

Vocal exercises that led her through major, minor, and modal scales.

Singing pop songs she liked and using them to learn reading skills.

Working on ear training exercises by using rhythmic solfege.

Having her play her class piano drills and relating them to the songs she was studying.

Learning the diction in her required literature (some early Italian songs) and using direct experiences[7] in which I spoke nothing but Italian to her for extended periods until she understood the translations before singing.

My objectives for her first year of study were to train her ears, brain, and body to feel and hear what she saw on the page because I knew her vocal apparatus would then follow along.

During her second year, Cindy has been assimilating all these new skills and beginning to learn literature quickly and accurately. Her technical development has also been rapid, although she tends to sing too "heavily" in the range from the tenth above middle C (E) to the twelfth above middle C (G),

causing her to sing under pitch. I have assigned her vocal exercises that call for her to "lighten" the sound by singing softer as she moves into her upper register, and we have performed many kinds of scales and harmonic exercises so she can learn to feel where she is within the scale (see Chapter 9, "Rhythmic Solfege").

She will perform her junior-level jury for all the voice faculty at the end of this semester, a jury she will have to pass in order to be allowed to enroll for upper-class credit. The jury includes sight-singing as well as acceptable performances of literature in English, Italian, and German.

We began the semester by discussing the jury requirements, then worked backward on the calendar, setting deadlines for when all music would be memorized (one month before the jury) and when all literature

---

[7]In this case, a direct experience would consist of me giving simple directions (e.g., touch your nose, point to your foot, stand up, sit down) in Italian (or German or French) with the student repeating the words while performing the action. This is very similar to the way children learn language, and helps the student "feel" the flow and natural rhythm of the language.

would be selected[8] (by the fifth week of the semester—the semester has sixteen weeks). Two weeks ago, she arrived with eleven compositions she thought were interesting, and we spent the lesson with Becky, her accompanist, flailing away at the piano as Cindy and I partly read/partly improvised our way through the pieces. The goal was to get the feel of the pieces (several were also new to me) and decide which might be used as the jury repertoire.

At last week's lesson, Cindy had brought in seven pieces she wanted to learn. We looked at the key and tempo relationships to make sure there was enough variety to make an interesting short program for the jury, since juries are treated as artistic performances at the university, and to ensure the literature and language requirements were fulfilled. Then Cindy, Becky, and I spoke, sang, danced, and played our way through the pieces. Together, we discussed which musical rules were applicable, used appropriate musical exercises, and looked for sections in which Cindy felt she might have technical problems. I asked her how she would analyze the problems and, of the exercises I have taught her, which ones might she use to solve the problems.[9] We will begin working on several of the pieces in more detail at today's lesson.

The Lesson Begins

Cindy and Becky arrive two minutes late and Cindy is in a state of agitation. She had a late-night fight with her boyfriend, a test in European history this morning, and a biology test immediately before her lesson. She announces she did not sleep very well and that she bombed the biology test and has no idea how she did on the history test. As I listen to her, I begin wondering if she will be able to concentrate during the lesson.

Becky is also a sophomore and, coincidentally, in the same biology class. Becky says the biology test was very hard and she didn't even finish. The two commiserate a bit and both become more irritated at the professor.

---

[8]This is the selection process I generally use:

a. Give the student a list of names of prominent composers who wrote in the period and language the student is studying and direct the student to the library or music store to browse through the literature. For the student who does not play piano—most do not—I suggest finding recordings of pieces by the composers on the list, or I play them myself as the student watches the score.

b. The student is directed to find a total of approximately twenty pieces that will comprise the reading repertoire; then the culling process begins. We start with student's affective responses to music and texts, gauge the student's technical skills vis-à-vis the technical requirements of a particular piece, and end with approximately ten pieces from which the memorized repertoire will be selected.

[9]Teaching the skills to analyze and solve problems is part of effective teaching.

Making Feelings Work for You

I ask Cindy to make a gesture with her arms that will show how she feels. After she makes the gesture, I ask Becky to make a gesture to show how she feels. Then I direct both of them to put the feeling in their faces, then in their voices and bodies. I perform their gestures with them to understand[10] what they are feeling. Soon the three of us are laughing.

Cindy announces she wants to work on *Vergebliches Ständchen* of Brahms because the "high F-sharps don't feel right" (she is using the A major version). I am not sure Cindy and Becky have moved past their irritation, so I ask them to perform the piece using the feelings they were experiencing and to show them with their faces and gestures.

◆ *Vergebliches Ständchen* **Op. 84, No. 4 by Johannes Brahms** ◆

Gu - ten a bend mein Schatz, gu - ten A - bend mein Kind

The performance has very little shading but a great deal of energy. We laugh again at the irritated young man in the song and the heated replies of the young lady. I think Cindy and Becky have moved past the feelings they brought with them, and are now able to concentrate.

Cindy says she felt better singing the piece this time, partly because she was paying attention to her feelings and not to the music (she became musically unconscious). Now she wants to be able to "feel good about singing it when I'm thinking about it."

Relating the Music to Movement

I ask if they know what a Ländler is. No. I demonstrate the heavy Ländler steps and then have them try them as I improvise a Ländler on the piano. They quickly understand the heavy crusis on all the beats, particularly the first beat of each measure.

I ask them to make the second beat of each measure the heaviest beat. They dance in that manner for a few seconds, then I call out "third beat" and play accordingly.

---

[10]Understanding cannot exist without being related to experience. Whether an event actually occurs or is imagined, when the brain causes the body to react, then the event is "experienced." I have watched moving pictures projected on 180-degree screens and experienced stomach-churning dives and knuckle-whitening flights as my body responded to what my eyes saw, even though my "rational" brain kept telling me I was safely seated in a theater.

I demonstrate the rhythmic pattern ♫| ♫ ♩| ♫ ♩| and ask them to join me as we move around the room feeling the weightiness of the note that follows shorter notes. After they have spent a few seconds on the exercise, I ask Cindy to speak the text as she moves around the room.

Learning to Analyze

She quickly realizes she has to stress the "bend" of *Abend* (measure 2) in order to match the musical stress[11] even though the spoken emphasis is *Abend*. I suggest that either Brahms made a mistake in setting the text, or he is trying to tell us something about the background and character of the young man (Er). We look at the girl's part (Sie) and find similar unusual stresses in *verschlossen* and *Mutter*.

Becky points out that the first beat of several measures seem to go up rather than down. She has realized that not all downbeats go down and, like the first beats in *Vergebliches Ständchen*, some actually go up. I play several measures as Becky and Cindy move around the room, some with downbeats (in this case using a quarter note on the first beat) and others with downbeats which go up (using rhythmic patterns that divide the first beat). Once again, they move around the room with Cindy reciting the text, feeling the upward moving quality of the so-called downbeats.

Returning to the text, I ask Cindy and Becky to think about why Brahms would distort some of the words—assuming he did so purposely. After some thought, they respond with answers like "maybe to show the people are kind of uncultured," "to show they're young and gawky," "it just makes it (the music) more interesting to kind of twist it around."

She and Becky perform again, this time paying attention to places where the music supports the natural accent or distorts it. At the end of the performance, I ask them what they learned that time, and listen as they talk about the need to overdo the stresses so they are clear; Cindy says she will go through her other jury literature to see how other composers followed or distorted natural accents.

I ask her how her "F-sharps" felt; she chuckled and said they felt good and that she was hardly paying attention to them because she was so involved with the accents and how they affected her characterization. I told her they sounded clearer and easier to me, but that she could modify the vowels on the F-sharp even more to further clarify the sound. I have her practice saying the word *Abend* as if it were "ab (^)nd" several times until she notices the small changes in feeling in her throat.

---

[11]There are two principles at work here: (1) a longer note after a series of shorter notes receives added weight (ref. the rule of subdivision); (2) in an intervallic leap of a fourth or greater, either up or down, the second note receives greater stress.

Once I am satisfied with the modification, I ask her to describe the physical effect. It is important that she be able to describe the feeling; I am aware of the action of the base of her tongue and the changes in space in her pharyngeal opening, but my knowledge of this is quite different than her experiencing the changes.

Next, I direct her to sing the F-sharp an octave lower than written to test the new feelings and, finally, to sing it as indicated in the score. As she sings it, I ask Becky to play the harmony so Cindy can hear how the F-sharp fits into the entire chord. She repeats the passage several times, attempting to reproduce the kinesthetic response.

Testing

At this point in the lesson, we turn to other literature and continue the analysis of how composers juxtapose spoken and musical accents. As the lesson continues, I am interested in observing how Cindy and Becky use their newly discovered information.

Summary

This lesson provides you one example of solving an apparent technical difficulty through musical means. In the case of *Vergebliches Ständchen*, Brahms had distorted the normative measure (normally **1** 2 3, **1** 23 into 1 **2** 3, 1 **2** 3) to achieve an artistic end. Discovering ways to experience this distortion through movement allowed Cindy's body to "teach her voice."

It would have been of little value for me to tell Cindy and Becky about the distortion, since I would have been giving them my perceptions of my physical sensations. No person can read another person's mind, nor can one person ever fully experience the physical sensations of another. As an Alexander teacher told me recently, "I do not live in *your* body." Understanding comes with experience, so Cindy and Becky had to have the experience before they could really understand the distortion.

LESSON WITH A FOURTH-YEAR STUDENT

Background

Manuel is a twenty-two-year-old undergraduate baritone in his fourth year of study with me. He is an outstanding student who plays jazz piano, is in the marching band, and has had leads in several campus musicals and operettas. This semester, in addition to singing the role of Ben in *The Telephone* (by Giancarlo Menotti), he is also giving a full recital.

He is working toward a degree in choral music education, and his career goals include teaching music in the public schools for a few years, probably as a high school choral director ("Just to try it out," he says), then returning to graduate school to earn a performance degree and see what the life of a professional singer might hold.

This lesson occurs approximately three weeks before his recital-approval jury. He has selected his repertoire using the process I described earlier, and has arrived at a program that includes three Handel arias, four lied of Brahms, three melodies by Debussy, four *Cabaret Songs* by William Bolcom, and three songs from *The House of Life* by Ralph Vaughan Williams, as well as selections from several musicals.

He has approached his learning using several of the musical exercises, analyzed the music using the musical rules, and memorized the texts through movement. We have already gained more insight into the literature by having Manuel sing the bass line of the accompaniment while Carl, the pianist who will accompany him, sang the melody and I recited the text using the dramatic indications given in the music.

The Lesson

Manuel arrives and announces his life is a bit hectic, but going well. He mentions that he has had some allergy problems, and we commiserate about the bane of allergies. I suggest that since he is physically not quite up to his usual standards, he might not be able to sing quite as softly or as slowly as he would like in several of the pieces he works on today.[12] He agrees that this might be a good idea.

Carl has not arrived yet, so I move to the piano and have Manuel perform several vocalises that are useful warm-ups when the vocal mechanism feels "thick." After performing several, he says he feels better, but his voice might be a "little touchy."

Organizing the Lesson Around Student Goals and Teacher Goals

Carl arrives, and he, Manuel, and I discuss what will be worked on in the lesson. I mention I want to hear the Brahms and Debussy groups to make

---

[12]My experience has been that many students automate their performance behavior without considering the varying conditions of their bodies or their surroundings. Consequently, they are surprised that today they cannot sing as loudly, softly, quickly, or slowly as they did yesterday, or that the room is drier, dustier, bigger, or smaller than they expected. Teaching students to respond to the environment, to use it rather than fight it, enhances their flexibility in performances.

sure the song order works in terms of key and tempo relationships and vocal endurance. Manuel and Carl mention they have had some disagreements about tempos in several of the pieces and want my reactions.

They decide to begin with the Debussy group. I ask them what will be most helpful: stopping between pieces or running an entire group and then going back? They choose the latter. So I sit at my desk and have a notepad ready to take notes during the performance. The notes will include remarks about score accuracy, diction, vocal technique, and descriptions of mood and movement that I might describe as vivid, hazy, flowing, uneasy, restful, and so on.

(I digress from the lesson for a moment to mention my expectation that they will continue the performance regardless of what happens. They have both been through improvisation exercises in the learning process that will enable them to proceed even if Manual forgets words, gets lost, or has a technical problem. They must now create the performance atmosphere.)[13]

I begin mentally reviewing the criteria for performance as Carl and Manuel take their performance positions, as well as pay attention to how they deal with the problem of creating a mood before the first notes are sounded. The performance opens with *Beau Soir*, then *Romance*, followed by *Mandoline*, and ending with *Les Cloches*.

I immediately note that the tempos need to be more clearly defined or the entire group will be performed in the same tempo even though the meters differ. I write other remarks that describe the tension I see in Manuel's left shoulder; the very nice subtle shift of his eyes, face, and body between the pieces that help change the mood; several diction mistakes; deft use of nuance in most of the pieces; fine balance between the piano and voice; the silky quality of Manuel's soft upper voice on "vapeur surnaturelle" in *Romance*.

Analyzing the Performance

I begin the critique by asking Manuel and Carl how they felt about the performance and hear "I felt a little stiff in that section. . . ." "I thought

---

[13]Research into learning has confirmed that we tend to perform better on tests when the tests are taken in the environment where the learning took place. Translated for performers, this means we will perform best if the learning takes place on stage, in front of an audience! Obviously we cannot have infinite access to auditoriums or audiences as we study our music, so it behooves us to create the performance environment in the studio and the practice room.

Yet, in training performers, we almost always teach and practice in an affective vacuum, so when the performer steps on stage in front of a live audience, it comes as an affective surprise. Finding ways to generate the adrenaline, concentration, distractions, and thrill of live performance in the studio and practice room needs to be a paramount task of the performer, at least in the final learning stages.

we were really together here . . ." "I started thinking about what you were writing, and forgot the words . . ." "I don't know what's going on in this section. Help!" We laugh about the vagaries of performance. I mention the chagrin I felt after a recital in which I sang an entire section of a Ravel piece in French gibberish when I forgot the words, only to be greeted backstage afterward by four French exchange students!

I quickly read my notes about the performance aloud, then give them to Manuel to take with him for review. I suggest we begin working on the opening of *Beau Soir*.

Analyzing and Problem Solving

I ask them to begin the piece again. I know that most disputes about tempo are not about speed, but about quality of beat, and I suspect this might be the case here. After several measures of a tug-of-war, I stop the performance and ask Carl to count aloud as he plays the opening.

◆ *Beau Soir* **by Claude Debussy** ◆

He counts "1 2 3, 1 2 3" very metacrusically. I ask him to count, "1 2 **3**, 1 2 **3**," saying "3" in a floating quality to understand that feeling. He immediately hears the change in the motion over the bar line, and says he likes it.

I ask Manuel to sing his first phrase a cappella and conduct himself as he sings the first phrase.

◆ *Beau Soir* **by Claude Debussy** ◆

Lorsque au soleil cou - chant les ri - viè - res sont ro - ses,

It is clear from his singing and movement that he is feeling each measure in one. I direct Carl and Manuel to link arms and each to move through the measure in his own way. Manuel takes one step per measure while Carl takes three; Carl tugs at Manuel and Manuel holds back, resisting the pull. The tempo dispute is made visible.

There is more laughter after several measures of this tugging and resisting. I direct them to reverse roles, Carl moving in one and Manuel in three. After several more reversals, I direct Manuel to sing the accompaniment pattern, while moving in three, and Carl to sing the voice line while moving in one.

Next, I direct Manuel to sing the vocal line as he puts the accompaniment pattern in his feet, and for Carl to sing the accompaniment pattern as he puts the rhythm of the vocal line in his feet; this is a very difficult assignment. They struggle with this for several measures until, as expected, they both fall apart.[14]

Testing

I am curious to see how much each has learned from the other. I ask them to return to the linked-arm position and each to sing his part while trying to incorporate ideas he has learned from the other. Their joint movement begins flowing without the previous tussle as each incorporates aspects of the other's movement. Neither has forced his ideas on the other, nor has he given up his own ideas, but, rather, their ideas have evolved into a new movement that combines the best of both.

However, another problem remains. Like most singers, when Manuel sings alone, he is rhythmically accurate, but when his two eighth notes are against the piano's triplets, he begins gliding through them so the listener does not experience the two against three movement.

---

[14]It is better to have experience and fail than never to have the experience because through our failures we explore our limitations and find ways to surmount them. We can learn from our successes, but we learn even more from our failures.

◆ *Beau Soir* by Claude Debussy ◆

To deal with this problem, I ask both Manuel and Carl to step a quarter note beat while clapping three times per beat. On the command, "change," they clap twice per beat. They can perform this task easily, so the new direction is to clap the quarter and perform the two, then the three, beats with their feet. When this becomes easy, I ask them to speak the words "one, two" while clapping three times per step. I join them as we play with this exercise, switching the patterns from voice, to feet, to hands, until we perform the task easily.

I ask Manuel to clap the quarter beat, step the triplets, and recite the text in the duples. This is a difficult task, and he stumbles—literally—a couple of times before he is able to make the three rhythmic elements work together. I ask Carl to try this and he has a great deal of difficulty, since he—a typical pianist—seldom moves to music and is fairly uncoordinated when moving through space. Manuel, watching Carl having problems, mentions he is "kind of glad to see you're having trouble too, since I was feeling like the proverbial 'dumb singer.'" Carl laughs.

We return to the performance as Carl and Manuel work to incorporate what they have just learned. They are successful some of the time and fumble other times, something I assume will happen, since its takes time and thought to incorporate new skills.

Transferring Ideas

After another performance in which they have more success, I ask Manuel if he wants to continue working on *Beau Soir* or move on to other pieces. He decides to change.

We explore the metaphors that Carl and Manuel have developed for each piece and discover both performers have quite different ideas. I introduced Manuel to the use of metaphor early in his studies with me because metaphor can provide an affective background to both the learning and performing processes.

Each describes and then plays or sings his metaphor for a particular piece. Then we search for ways to combine the two metaphors until they arrive at shared perceptions about the affective intent of the piece. They perform the Brahms group, and it is clear a similar process would work there and, indirectly, they discover ways to organize their practice times together.

Carl and Manuel have realized they need to talk about their perceptions of the music without constantly playing and singing. If, for example, they sit at a table and discuss the music and chant their way through the pieces, they will accomplish more in an hour than in three hours of playing and singing.[15]

Summary

The process of Manuel's lesson included the following:

- ◆ Having the students as full partners in organizing the lesson time and setting goals.
- ◆ Creating a performance climate by continuing to work through difficulties without stopping.
- ◆ Analyzing what worked, and what did not work, in the performance.
- ◆ Defining the possible problem, developing a way to solve the problem, then testing the solution.
- ◆ Transferring newly learned abilities to other pieces to see if they work there also.
- ◆ Developing ways to organize practice time.

---

[15]Playing or singing the pitches constantly can distract from learning the music. In order to learn music well, we must internalize it; focusing on the external sound distracts from this internalizing process.

SUMMARY

I believe that for effective teaching, the following concepts and processes need to occur in various degrees in all lessons.

1. The students are recognized as full partners in organizing the lesson time and setting goals. They are also made aware of their learning processes. Teacher and student work together to structure the learning. The teacher is responsible for setting the standards and, in institutional settings, making the student aware of curriculum requirements. For example, in a typical lesson in my studio, I begin the lesson by asking the student what she wants to know or be able to do by the end of the lesson. After hearing the student's answer, I then add my own plans, such as, "I want to hear the Brahms, especially that passage we worked on last week." Thus the lesson is quickly structured and both the student and I have contributed.

Students involved in structuring their learning learn more, and the teacher who shares the authority does not lose authority, but shares the role of "teacher" with the student. Sharing authority also releases the teacher from maintaining the facade of having godlike wisdom and knowledge. I believe that ideally the teacher becomes a co-learner with the student.

2. The teacher encourages the students to bring their emotions and personal experiences to the music. This raises the issue once again of assigning music and text that is beyond the physical and emotional understanding of the student. All too frequently at auditions and competitions, I hear high school and college undergraduates singing pieces that would physically and emotionally tax thirty-year-olds. A century ago, Jaques-Dalcroze deplored the fact that teachers assign music to students that is beyond their ken. Unfortunately, the practice continues.

Robert Abramson gives an example of this. During a workshop for pianists he gave in California, he was working with a young girl who was performing a Chopin nocturne in a very errhythmic manner. He was unable to make the changes he wanted, and in exasperation he said, "Can't you remember what it's like being passionately in love and losing that love? Remember the heartbreaking sense of loss that comes over you when you look back at it?"

The girl looked at him and said, "I don't know what you mean. I'm only twelve years old!"

3. The music is related to affect from the first stages of learning. When words are used to describe the music and feelings about the music, the student is encouraged to explore a broad range of emotional and musical shadings. Examples of words that describe music might include bouncy, light, floating, gliding, skipping (notice these are descriptions of qualities of motion); affective words might include angry, elated, melancholy, bitter, joyous.

Occasionally, technique might be highlighted or the score approached in a piecemeal manner to check for accuracy, but this process should be brief because it can be devitalizing.

4. A performance climate is created in the studio. Rather than working in an emotional vacuum, students are encouraged to create metaphors while learning the music, and to focus on what they want the audience to experience during the performance. During a lesson, before students sing a piece they have prepared, I often ask, "What do you want me to listen for as you sing?" This question encourages students to (1) remember someone is listening and (2) focus attention on the effect of their sound on the audience rather than the production of the sound. A Dalcrozian says, "Let me know by your performance how I should move to the music you are making."

Additionally, experiencing the various elements that will occur in the actual performances will both improve concentration during practice and lessen the anxiety felt before performances. In an ideal world, all lessons and practice would occur in the setting in which the performance will actually occur.

5. Music teaches music. I believe that in a well-taught lesson, the teacher speaks as little as possible. When the teacher does speak, it is to give an analysis of what was just sung or to encourage the student to analyze the performance. But most of the time the teacher can give the analysis by recreating the sound or showing how the teacher would move if dancing the sound. Graphically or aurally demonstrating produces quicker, more lasting results than using words. For example, if the student reads the poetry in a deadened voice, the teacher demonstrates the deadened voice and then reads in a lively manner. Telling the student his voice was dead might change his performance slightly; showing the student will change his performance quickly.

In the ideal lesson, the teacher becomes the music through the use of voice, face, and gesture, and the environment in the studio becomes a musical environment.

6. Vocal technique and technical studies are not slighted, but placed within a musical context. All technical studies can be placed within a rhythmic and harmonic context.

For example, the faithful old exercise

may be rhythmically changed into

while the piano provides the harmony that might be as simple as

or more complicated:

or:

In this manner, the teacher teaches technique but always within a musical context.

7. The students learn to analyze their work. Most students practice poorly because they cannot analyze their work in the practice room; when they have a problem, they simply wait for the next lesson and assume the teacher will fix it. This is one reason why most students accomplish so little from week to week. If the students can learn to define the problem, develop a way to solve the problem, then test the solution, they will have taken a giant step toward becoming artists capable of making their own decisions.

If the lesson includes a performance, helping the student analyze what worked and what did not work will also teach discrimination and reduce performance anxiety. Learning to describe the performance rather than evaluating the performance is very important during the analytical process. The educational system teaches us to evaluate (good, bad, mediocre, excellent, terrible), but not to describe ("I was under pitch in these measures . . . I performed these very well . . . I forgot the words here."). Performance anxiety occurs because the performer imagines the worst possible outcome ("I might forget the words"), then evaluates it ("I will look stupid").

8. Transferring newly learned abilities to other pieces to see if they work there also. When the teacher has taught the Italian "gl" in the word "imbroglio," then has to teach it again in "gli," and again in "glielo," then the student is not transferring learning. Students are excited when they learn to transfer a new skill or understanding from one piece to another because there is a sense of being in control, and learning becomes an interesting challenge rather than an odious task. In addition, the teacher is less frustrated when the students begin to transfer learning because the teacher does not have to teach the same lesson over and over.

9. Developing ways to organize practice time. We voice teachers tend to assume that students somehow know how to practice. We expect people to practice and be discerning at the same time when, in fact, they need an expert sitting beside them to not only make the corrections, but suggest directions. When practicing alone, seldom does a student say, "I'm having trouble with this. Why am I having trouble with this? How can I change it?" Rather, they wait for the teacher to provide the critique and solve problems. While they are willing to accept the teacher's guidance, they often do not know how they make the changes and solve the problems. Experimenting with solutions leads to artistic independence and should be encouraged.

Each lesson provides us with the opportunity to train our students to be musically intelligent, to use their imaginations and analytical abilities in new ways as they develop their techniques and musical skills. I believe the best teachers do not, in fact, teach music; instead they teach students how to learn music.

Robert Abramson once said that after a lesson his first question is, "After thirty minutes with me, do you feel more aware, more alive, have more questions? Are you quickened to work at something, and do you have more skills to work with? That's my question and it helps me to know whether or not I have taught a good lesson."

◆ Chapter 14 ◆

conclusion

One of my acquaintances, a gifted performer, works as a high school choral director. He recently told me about a recurring nightmare that has become more intense over the years.

In his dream, he walks into a rehearsal with a high school choir that is new to him. This is the first of twenty-five rehearsals he will have to prepare for a concert. He sits down at the piano and begins his usual vocal warm-ups and is immediately elated to hear his ideal choral sound coming from the choir. He continues the warm-ups and discovers the group can do anything he asks of them technically.

He hands out the music, and begins the rehearsal with the simplest composition. The choir reads the score with absolute accuracy. He moves to a more difficult piece; again the ensemble reads it accurately. Eventually he has had the ensemble read all the music for the concert, and they have read with unerring accuracy, including the pieces in German and French.

At this point in his dream, he breaks into a cold sweat because for years he has had to teach the rhythms, the pitches, diction, and technique, and now, suddenly, he is standing in front of an ensemble that does not have to be taught any of these things: he has twenty-four rehearsals and nothing to teach! "I've been so busy teaching the basic skills, I woke up terrified that I've forgotten how to teach music," he said.

Like my friend the conductor, voice teachers and student performers often become so bogged down with the obvious need to "fix notes," build technique, or teach "pieces" that we forget the music is not in the pitches or the technique. Having a good technique, learning a score accurately, and having excellent diction are all necessary attributes for a successful singer, but they must all be directed toward a common end: the expression of human emotion through the medium of music.

I have tried to show how musical considerations have a direct effect on technique. The illustration which follows demonstrates some of the elements that need to be taken into consideration in the performance of a "simple" quarter note.

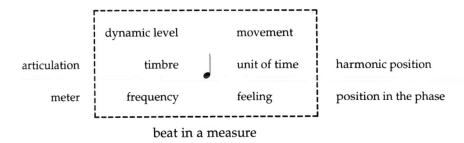

articulation

meter

beat in a measure

Transform that symbol into

and other questions must be asked if it is to be performed in an expressive manner:

◆ What is the dynamic level?

◆ What is the articulation (how is it attacked, sustained, released)?

◆ How was it approached (by a step, a half step, a larger skip; from above, from below)?

◆ Where is it in the scale (I in A-Flat major, iii in F minor, IV in E-Flat major, vi in C minor—there are at least twelve possibilities)?

◆ What is the meter and where does the note come in a measure?

◆ Where does the note occur in the phrase?

◆ What affect motivated the sound (anger, lust, suspicion, giddiness, etc.)?

While the technical skills for singing have developed steadily over the years, teachers and critics have noted that vocal performances become more emotionally sterile with each passing year. More and more concerts are becoming displays of admirable technical prowess that leave audiences emotionally anesthetized, and they leave such concerts remarking on the "high notes," the "bigness" (or "smallness") of the voice, the flexibility, the legato, followed by the question, Where shall we go for dessert? Nothing has happened affectively to the audience; they leave unchanged, unmoved. The medium has become the message: what you hear (a pretty voice and good technique) is all you get.

The values, principles, and methodology developed by Jaques-Dalcroze one hundred years ago is an antidote to this emotional narcolepsy. By applying the principles and methodology described in this book, we can begin to deal with musical problems without having to resort to a coach.

I believe a major strength of the Dalcroze methodology is its concern with teaching musical behavior more than teaching any specific musical technique: Dalcroze-oriented voice teachers or performers are more interested in teaching and learning how to hear, think, feel, and behave like musicians than simply performing pieces.

Other tenets of the methodology that have been explored in this book are these:

◆ The raison d'être of Western music is to express emotion.

◆ We experience emotions physically and can train our bodies to transform internal reactions into external motion, motion that can be perceived by the listener.

◆ To live, music must have perceived qualities of motion. If the listener does not perceive various qualities of motion, then the performance is dead.

◆ If all music begins with human motion (taking a breath, pressing a valve, and so on), then the most effective way to learn and study music is to experience the qualities of motion with the body. The performer learns the "dance" of the music in the practice room, internalizes that "dance," then can stand quietly during the performance and make the hearts and souls of the audience dance and sway. "Feelings" are closely linked to movement. The power of singing comes not from beautiful or massive sounds, but from the ability of the performer to make the listener feel.

◆ Music teaches music. Music is not about words (talk about music), but sounds that are organized with the intent of expressing emotion. The teacher who is able to use few words and much music will probably produce musical students.

◆ As teachers, if, in fact, we are training artistic behavior, then we must model that behavior for our students. It is not enough for the teacher to tell the student how to perform. He or she must use voice, face, and gestures to indicate the desired effects. We must be able to teach technique and literature, but if Western music is an expression of emotion, then we must not lose sight of the higher goal of assisting our students to express their emotions musically. Good teaching is a performing art.

◆ As students and performers, our job is to learn what the composers have indicated in their scores and to develop the technical skills to interpret the music to the audience. We can give the audience the basic "dashes and dots," but the audience wants to know what those dashes and dots mean. When we convey that meaning through our sounds, when the audience perceives our sounds as organized and moving, then we have become expressive performers.

Where will you go from here? I have given an overview of the Dalcroze methodology and examples of how you might apply it. Often while learning a new approach, teachers and performers will feel betwixt and between an old way of teaching and learning and a new, not-quite-integrated approach. As we struggle to incorporate new thinking into our behaviors, we often develop amnesia: we forget that we are intelligent, imaginative, and experienced teachers and performers already.

When I stumbled on Dalcroze ideas, I had been singing professionally for six years and teaching voice at the university level for twelve years: I had also conducted professionally for eighteen years: I was a very experienced musician. The effects of the Dalcroze approach on my performance were immediate and obvious to me and my colleagues; the effects on my students' performances became apparent over the course of several semesters. However, when I had lessons with Robert Abramson I sometimes felt as if I had returned to kindergarten, as if I did not have a musical bone in my body! This was not Abramson's fault. It was because I developed amnesia! In pursuing new skills, working to incorporate new thinking, I forgot what I knew.

When I give workshops in the Dalcroze method, teachers tell me they have similar feelings of incompetence. I am certainly sympathetic, so I remind them, as I am reminding you: you have a wealth of knowledge and experience to add to the ideas presented in this book. Consider these ideas as guides to examining, adding to, and enhancing skills you already possess: ponder them, experiment with them, change them, and, most of all, enjoy them.

questions

and

answers

If I really start using this stuff in my teaching (moving around the studio, etc.) will my students think I'm crazy?

Yes. Next question.

You wrote about learning pieces in a boring way. Aren't there some pieces that *are* boring?

Yes. However, most truly boring, cliché-ridden pieces fall by the musical wayside and die a natural death of neglect unless discovered and put on life support by a musicologist in search of a project. Even the great composers wrote some real stinkers, but even they (the compositions, not the composers) can be given interesting performances—once.

Part of my rationale for writing this book is that I am very tired of hearing interesting, life-filled music performed in a boring manner.

If I really believe the ideas presented in this book, does that mean I have been teaching the wrong things over the years? Does that mean I have been teaching poorly?

As the song says, "It ain't necessarily so." Remember, the Dalcroze system is descriptive, not prescriptive: I am more interested in having you think about and explore new ways to teach, and what to teach, than giving you three hundred little "tricks" to use. You might have already been addressing many of the issues in the book, but called them by other names. If not, then think about them!

Also, the musical behavior of our students tells us a great deal about the effectiveness of our teaching: how well do they perform, and how expressively? How do they feel about their performing? Do they love making music over the years, even if they are not "professionals"?

Several years ago, an internationally renowned conservatory polled its graduates and discovered almost 90 percent of them were *not* making their living in music, dance, or theater. Other major conservatories have arrived at similar statistics with other polls. The reasons for these statistics vary, but they seem to fall into two categories:

1. The small musical "market" and lack of money to support the arts.
2. "Burnout" from overpractice and feelings of intense competitiveness.

Many of the 90-percent also reported they were no longer interested in making music! It had become too much of a struggle with too many bad feelings; they had lost their love for music.

Having students become professional performers ought not be the sole criteria of success for the teacher. I think our society needs a musical populace, people who have music in their homes and participate in an active musical life in their communities. To me, my success as a teacher lies in the answers to these questions:

◆ Do my former students look back on our time together with good feelings of having been challenged and a sense of accomplishment?
◆ Did they leave my tutelage loving music and performing as much or more than when we began our work together?
◆ Do they still make music in their homes and communities, as well as the concert halls?

If, when I ask these questions, I receive mostly affirmatives, then I believe I am justified in feeling successful as a teacher.

What about the frustration a student might have learning music this way?

Present-day teaching wisdom says, do not allow students to be frustrated because, as everybody knows, frustration is bad. Everyone knows learning has to be developed in easy stages or Johnny will get mad and quit because Johnny does not know how to control his emotions! Everyone knows a good teacher does not allow the student to become frustrated. I wonder if those same teachers have seen those same students struggling to learn a new task that is important to them, like learning to drive? So long as the students perceive the task as important to them, for their own reasons, they will continue the struggle. Who is this ubiquitous "everyone"?

Life is hard, and life is sometimes frustrating. We will give our students a great gift if we can teach them to be aware of their feelings and then to control and direct those feelings. During a lesson, when a student looks at me and says, in a critical tone, " I'm getting *frustrated*!" I respond (in my most innocent tone), "Can you feel frustrated and still work?" I have never yet had a student say no. I am giving students the opportunity to learn to be in control of emotions rather than allowing the emotions to control them.

I hasten to add that I do not deliberately want to create frustration, but I *do* want to make the task a challenge for the student's skills. Otherwise the student will learn nothing.

◆ Appendix A ◆

suggestions for learning
a score
musically

EXERCISES DISTILLED FROM CHAPTER 11

1. Read the text (or a translation of the text if one is available). What mood or emotion do you experience? Describe the moods or emotions you feel.

2. Examine the composer's tempo markings (andante, largo, allegro, rallentando, etc.), dynamic markings, fermatas, sudden high or low notes. What do they tell you about the composer's feelings about the text?

3. Speak the text in a dramatic fashion, as in a public performance. How many times did you breath? What pitch range did you use in your speaking? Find your speaking pitches on the piano. Repeat the exercise and increase the range of the spoken pitches. Translate the text into your own words. Recite the text again using an emotion or attitude selected at random. How did the randomly selected attitude highlight or contrast the feelings in the text?

4. Speak the text following the melodic line, out of rhythm, using the musical rules.

5. Speak the text in the rhythm of the music, being careful to vary pitch and dynamics, following the musical rules and the normative measure. What types of articulation were used? Pay attention to the phrasing of the text as it relates to the phrasing of the music.

6. If you can, play the accompaniment in chords out of rhythm, as you sing the melody. Roll (i.e., arpeggiate) the chords so you can hear all the notes.

7. Sing the piece using all the expressive elements just listed.

You may assume you will not be able to keep all of the expressive elements working during the first attempts to sing the piece. Usually the rhythmic vitality diminishes and the body becomes dead because you might be concerned about the physical technique and confused by the sounds of the notes.

Find ways to keep your body alive and moving, and to attend to the musical rules of expression. It will take several attempts for you to coordinate all the skills.

You will notice that many technical problems begin to resolve themselves as you synthesize the skills.

BONUS EXERCISE FOR NON-PIANO PLAYERS

Sit at a table or some other hard surface, and imagine the table is your keyboard.

Begin by playing the prominent rhythms of the left hand, being sure to move your hand left and right as the music indicates.

Do the same with your right hand separately.

Play both hands together. Be sure to observe all the diacritical markings (accel, rit., fermatas, cres., etc.).

Play just the left hand as you speak the rhythms of your vocal line ("scat," the syllables used by jazz singers, works nicely for this exercise).

Do the same as you play just your right hand.

Feeling pretty good? Then play both hands together as you "scat" your line.

Feeling courageous? Rather than "scatting," speak the written text in rhythm as you play both hands.

If you are feeling adventurous, play your solo line as you sing one of the hands of the piano part.

After you have worked through most or all of the preceding exercises, close the score. Can you still feel the rhythms you just played? The goal is to understand as much of the piano part as possible and experience how the lines intermingle.

LIST OF ATTITUDES

Make a set of flash cards with one attitude on each card. The flash cards will prove helpful in developing an affective matrix for practice and performance.

arrogant	proud	cowardly
brave	excited	dejected
bubbly	sensual	bold
eager	longing	relieved
ecstatic	haughty	humble
giddy	angry	happy
melancholy	confused	sadly
passionate	penitent	avaricious
pious	fervent	remorseful
sexy	lustful	suspicious
vengeful	cynical	sarcastic
vindictive	hopeful	ardent

◆ Appendix B ◆

Greenwell registration chart

INTRODUCTION

In the last years of his life, Gean Greenwell constructed a registration chart based on his many years of experience teaching voice. He had an extraordinary ability to analyze voices and was able to explain, often humorously, what he heard, and was a strong believer that efficient registration cured many technical problems.

He had given the chart to several of his older students, myself included, and had asked us to field-test it for him. He was aware that it was in a rudimentary stage and was hoping to add refinements but was unable to do so.

The most important aspect of studying how a master teacher works is to learn to hear as the teacher hears. Greenwell generously allowed my colleagues from Central Michigan University and me to audit his lessons and understand how he heard. A chart cannot impart that knowledge, but I hope you will find it and the accompanying information useful.

ELEMENTS OF REGISTRATION

How and when a singer moves from one register to another is determined by:
- ◆ the dynamics (how loud or soft) of the line.
- ◆ the vowel being sung at the time.
- ◆ whether the vocal line is ascending or descending, and whether the higher note(s) was approached by step or by leap.
- ◆ the musical and emotional effect the singer wants to give the audience.

The Register Chart gives examples of where register changes typically occur on the (a) vowel sung *forte*. Singing at quieter levels generally causes the upper registers to enter sooner.

Greenwell used vowel modification and assumed even untrained singers would modify to some degree, so the (a) in the upper registers was only approximate. The register transitions are based on a dynamic of forte, on an "ah" vowel.

◆ Register Chart ◆

The register transitions are based on a dynamic of forte, on an "ah" vowel.

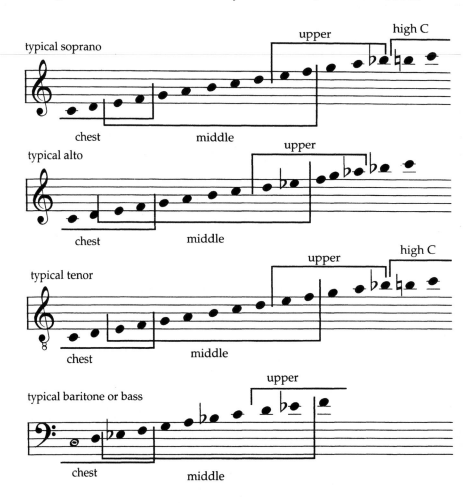

The overlapping lines indicated on the chart indicate those pitches which may be performed in a higher or lower register, depending on the direction of the vocal line. For example, look at the soprano portion of the chart and you will see the E and F above middle C are bracketed. If the soprano were singing a line like:

she would be advised to sing the F in the chest register. If the line were:

she would be advised to sing the E in the middle register.

Of course, whether she would follow these guides is dependent on the other elements listed above, dynamic, vowel, and so on.

The Register Chart is based on the dynamic being forte and the "ah" vowel. But what about the other vowels? The chart is presented below.

Whole notes indicate lower voice; solid notes indicate upper voice

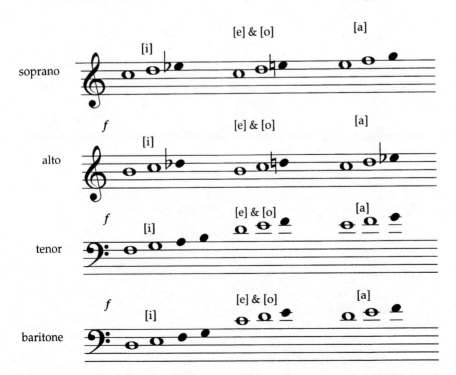

The next issue is: how do you tell one register from another? It is easiest to describe what happens to the sound when the singer does not shift registers appropriately. Some rules of thumb are:

1. *When a lower register is carried to high, the sound becomes harsh, "yelly" (a Greenwell term), and the singer cannot get softer (diminuendo) without the voice "breaking."* There are also accompanying physical signs of effort and discomfort such as muscles in the neck and throat looking strained. Tiredness and hoarseness also occur quickly, and there are complaints of "I can't sing that high."

2. *When a higher register is carried too low, the sound becomes breathy and the singer cannot get louder (crescendo), regardless of how much breath he or she uses.* Vocal fatigue can occur because of efforts to increase the amount of sound by "pushing" the voice.

3. *The "I can't" comments from the singer are signs of poor register shifting.*

   Mezzo soprano: "I can't sing above the G (above middle C) . . ."

   She is stuck in her chest register and not shifting to her middle register.

   Soprano: "I can't sing above that E (the 10th above middle C) . . ."

   She is stuck in her middle register and not shifting to her upper register.

   Soprano: "I can't sing very loudly below an E (above middle C) . . ."

   She is stuck in her middle register and not shifting into her chest register.

   Tenor: "I can't sing above an F (the 4th above middle C—the male voice being an octave lower than the female) . . ."

   He is stuck in his middle register and not shifting to his upper register.

   Tenor: "I can't sing anything below an E (6th below middle C) . . ."

   He is stuck in his middle register and not shifting into his chest register.

   Baritone/Bass: "I can't sing above a C (middle C) without cracking . . ."

   Care to guess?

bibliography

Abramson, Robert M. *Rhythm Games for Perception and Cognition*. Miami, FL: C.P.P. Belwin, 1973.

Balk, H. Wesley. *Performing Power: A New Approach for the Singer-Actor*. Minneapolis: University of Minnesota Press, 1985.

Bandler, Grinder. *Frogs Into Princes: Neuro Linguistic Programming* .™ New York: Carl Fischer, 1988.

Caldwell, Timothy. "A Dalcroze Perspective on Skills for Learning Music." *Music Educators Journal*, 79 (7): 1993.

Caldwell, Timothy. *Dalcroze Eurhythmics with Robert Abramson*. Videotape, Chicago: G.I.A. Publications, 1992.

Campbell, Joseph. *Creative Mythology—The Masks of God*. New York: Viking Penguin, 1968.

Choksy, Abramson, and Gillespie, Woods. *Teaching Music in the Twentieth Century*. Englewood Cliffs, NJ: Prentice Hall, 1986.

Christiani, Adolph F. *The Principles of Expression in Pianoforte Playing* (reprint of 1885 ed.). New York: Da Capo Press, 1974.

Coffin, Berton. *Sounds of Singing*. Metuchen, NJ: Scarecrow Press, 1987.

Cooper, Morton. *Change Your Voice, Change Your Life*. New York: Macmillan, 1984.

Doscher, Barbara M. *The Functional Unity of the Singing Voice*. Metuchen, NJ: Scarecrow Press, 1988.

Duckworth, Guy. *Handbook for Group Environments*. Unpublished document, Boulder, CO: University of Colorado, 1980.

Fields, Alexander. *Training the Singing Voice*. New York: Kings Crown Press (subsidiary of Columbia University Press), 1947.

Foote, Jeffrey. *The Vocal Performer: Development Through Science and Imagery.* Mount Pleasant, MI: Wildwood Music, 1989.

Gallwey, W. Timothy. *The Inner Game of Tennis.* New York: Random House, 1974.

Garcia, Manuel, II. *A Complete Treatise on the Art of Singing,* Parts I and II Collected, translated, and edited by Donald V. Paschlie. New York: Da Capo Press, 1975.

Green, Barry. *The Inner Game of Music.* Minneapolis: University of Minnesota Press, 1986.

Günter, Horst. "Mental Concepts in Singing: A Psychological Approach, Part 1." *The NATS Journal,* 48 (5): 1992.

Jaques-Dalcroze, Emile. *Rhythm, Music and Education.* Translated by Harold F. Rubenstein. New York: Putnam Press, 1921.

Lakeoff, George, and Johnson, Mark. *Metaphors We Live By.* Chicago: University of Chicago Press, 1980.

Lussy, Mathis M. *Musical Expression, Accents, Nuances, and Tempo, in Vocal and Instrumental Music.* Translated by M. E. von Glehn. New York: Macmillan Publications, 1986.

Martin, Frank. *Emile Jaques-Dalcroze—L'Homme, le Compositeur, le Crétur de la Rhythmique.* Leipzig: Neuchâtel, 1965. Unpublished translation by Robert Abramson, New York.

Miller, Richard. *The Structure of Singing: System and Art in Vocal Technique.* New York: Schirmer Books, 1986.

Mueller-Maerlei, Ruth. *Rules for Musical Expression.* Unpublished manuscript. New York.

Seitz, Jay. "I Move . . . Therefore I Am." *Psychology Today,* March/April 1993, pp. 50–55.

Spector, Irwin. *Rhythm and Life: The Work of Emile Jaques-Dalcroze.* Dance and Music Series No. 3. Stuyvesant, NY: Pendragon Press, 1990.

Vennard, William. *Singing, the Mechanism and the Technic.* New York: Carl Fischer, 1967.

Webster's New Collegiate Dictionary. Springfield: G. & C. Merriam Company, 1974.

◆ Index ◆